THE SECRET SAYINGS OF JESUS

by Robert M. Grant
in collaboration with
David Noel Freedman

With an English Translation
of the Gospel of Thomas
by William R. Schoedel

BARNES
& NOBLE
BOOKS
NEW YORK

This edition published by Barnes & Noble, Inc.,
by arrangement with Doubleday & Co., Inc.
a division of Bantam Doubleday Dell.

1993 Barnes & Noble Books

ISBN 1-56619-274-9
Printed and bound in the United States of America

M 9 8 7

CONTENTS

5

PREFACE

The newly discovered Gospel of Thomas is an important addition to early Christian literature, and it deserves a fairly thorough study so that it can be set in its proper context. It belongs to a collection of thirteen volumes of Gnostic papyri discovered near the modern village of Nag Hammadi (close to the ancient Chenoboskion), Egypt, in about 1945. Publication has been slow chiefly because of legal problems related to the ownership of the various volumes. Since 1948 descriptions and some excerpts from the papyri have been provided, chiefly by Doresse and Puech, but, as late as 1959, most of the documents remain unpublished.

There has been a good deal of controversy over the question of just who has discovered what in this collection. Certainly those who first worked with Togo Mina, director of the Coptic Museum before his death in 1949, made the first discoveries. These scholars were H.-C. Puech of Paris and his pupil Jean Doresse. And, as far as the correlation of the Coptic documents with other early Gnostic writings is concerned, the work of Puech remains incomparable. On the other hand, the recognition of the importance of the Gospel of Truth is due to Gilles Quispel, as is the remarkable effort he exerted to acquire the volume containing it for the Jung Institute. There is so much material awaiting exegesis that time should not be spent on adjusting claims for scholarly priority.

In this study we obviously cannot consider the various unpublished documents. Instead, we are going to examine the one treatise which lies closest to early Christianity in general—the Gospel of Thomas. Doresse looked through this gospel in the spring of 1949 and later announced that it was a "Gnostic composition which has no relation to the Christian apocryphal document concerning the infancy of Jesus . . . but perhaps corresponds to the work used by the Naassenes and by the Manichees." By 1952 Puech had discovered that Greek fragments of the same work had been found, many years earlier, among the Oxyrhynchus papyri but had never been correctly identified. By 1954 he had found another parallel, this time on a fragment of a shroud from Oxyrhynchus. In 1957 he published a thorough study of the gospel at Paris and also prepared an extremely important study of "Gnostic gospels and related documents" for a German edition of the apocryphal gospels.[1] The same year saw the publication of a brief study of Thomas by the Coptic scholar G. Garitte and an analysis of "the parables of the kingdom" by Garitte and Lucien Cerfaux.

In 1958 the first complete translation of Thomas appeared; it had been made from the photographs of Pahor Labib's edition by the German scholar Johannes Leipoldt. Finally, in 1959, Doresse published a study of the gospel which consists of a long introduction, a new translation, and a commentary.[2]

The present study was completed, in its original form, before the publication of Doresse's work, though it has

[1] For details on these publications and others, see the Select Bibliography.
[2] All citations of Doresse hereafter refer to this study, for details of which, see the Select Bibliography.

8

been revised throughout in order to take Doresse's obser-
vations into account. The translation of the Gospel of
Thomas which is used here was made from Coptic in May
1959 by William R. Schoedel of The University of Chicago.
The numbering system for the sayings in the gospel is that
of Leipoldt.

The translations from the Bible are not derived from
standard English versions but are based on Greek texts (in
one case—Isaiah 28:10—on Hebrew). In some instances
the same passage is translated in different ways for different purposes. In translations from the papyri, open brackets
indicate that the rest of a line is illegible; closed brackets
indicate that what is between them has been supplied by
conjecture. In the Gospel of Thomas, parentheses enclose
words supplied to fill out the sense apparently intended
by the Coptic; brackets indicate restorations; and pointed
brackets show that the text has been emended.

We shall see that, although the Gospel of Thomas is
almost certainly based on our gospels, along with other
materials chiefly Gnostic, it can provide us with a good
deal of insight into the ways in which early Christians and
Gnostics understood the teaching of Jesus. It contains a
valuable reflection of a part of his message—though this
part needs to be corrected by the apostolic gospel as a
whole.

ABBREVIATIONS USED IN THE NOTES

CRAcInscr	Comptes rendus de l'Académie des Inscriptions et Belles-Lettres (Paris)
H. E.	Historia Ecclesiastica (Church History)
PG	Patrologia Graeca (ed., J. P. Migne)
PL	Patrologia Latina (ed., J. P. Migne)
P. Oxy.	Oxyrhynchus Papyrus
RHR	Revue de l'histoire des religions (Paris)
TLZ	Theologische Literaturzeitung (Leipzig)
TU	Texte und Untersuchungen zur Geschichte der altchristlichen Literatur (Leipzig-Berlin)

palacios

THE SECRET SAYINGS OF JESUS

I

THE NEW DISCOVERY

Less than a dozen years ago the world of Bible students and scholars was shaken by the discovery of the Dead Sea Scrolls in the caves near Qumran. These scrolls took the Hebrew text of much of the Old Testament a millennium farther back and illuminated the Jewish background of the New Testament as it had not been illuminated before. Discovery was soon followed by publication, and by repeated new discoveries. Almost certainly, the community which lived in the monastery above the Dead Sea consisted of Essenes, a sect previously known only from the rather vague descriptions provided by three first-century writers, the Hellenized Jews Philo and Josephus and the Roman antiquarian and ethnologist Pliny. Now modern students could read what the Essenes themselves wrote. They could learn of the sect's passionate dislike of the priesthood in Jerusalem, of its founder, the Teacher of Righteousness, of its expectation of divine aid in a future holy war against the Romans. They could gain fresh insight into the vivid eschatological hopes of the Essenes. They could see how the sect reinterpreted the Old Testament in relation to its hopes and to the story of the Teacher. They could read its austere Manual of Discipline. And they could see how similar to the Essenes some early Christians, especially those of Jerusalem, had been. Renewed emphasis came to be laid on the origins of Christianity within Judaism—and specifically within "heterodox" Judaism. Indeed, there were those who argued that both John the Baptist and Jesus had been Essenes, and a few who held that the Christian interpretation of Jesus's crucifixion was based on that of the crucified Teacher of Righteousness. (Since there is no evidence that the Teacher was crucified, this idea is not remarkably convincing.)

What happened to the Essenes? Many of them were killed when the Romans sacked Qumran in A.D. 68; others doubtless became Christians, more or less orthodox, recognizing that the Messiah had already come. Others lost all hope for victory in this world, and came to recognize that essentially they were spiritual beings imprisoned here below in bodies. Their salvation could come only when the divine spirit or spark escaped to its spiritual home above. The road to escape lay in self-knowledge, recognition of the spark.

When such people transferred their hopes from earth to heaven, they created a religious movement known as Gnosticism, which flourished in the early centuries of our era. Similar movements are not unknown even today.

Even before the Qumran discoveries were made, a startling collection of Gnostic documents had been unearthed in Egypt, in about 1945. Far up the river Nile, near a village called Nag Hammadi, some peasants happened upon a large earthen jar in which were contained no fewer than thirteen leather-bound volumes of papyrus manuscripts. These manuscripts, written in Coptic during the fourth century of our era, contained forty-nine treatises which reflected the thought of several Gnostic groups. The peasants sold most of the lot for three Egyptian pounds, and it eventually reached Cairo, where—after a long sequence of difficulties—twelve volumes finally became the property of the Coptic Museum. One volume was acquired by a Belgian antiquities dealer named Eid; this was sold in 1952 to Gilles Quispel for the Jung Institute in Zurich. Quispel was acting on behalf of an American philanthropist, who ultimately presented the volume to the famous Swiss psychologist C. G. Jung on his eightieth birthday. It was an appropriate gift, for Jung has long been interested in Gnostic thought and its relation to the archetypes found in his own system. The present seems to have cost more than ten thousand dollars.

In 1956 three scholars—Malinine, Puech, and Quispel—published the most important document in the Jung Codex. This was the Gospel of Truth, previously known only from a couple of allusions to it made by the Church Fathers. This gospel is a mystical, meditative, homiletical treatment of themes derived partly from our gospels and partly from heterodox Jewish speculations. As the Fathers point out, it is completely unlike the Church's gospels. Its subject is not Jesus himself but the meaning of the salvation which he revealed.

For New Testament studies a more significant publication, in the same year, was that produced by Dr. Pahor Labib, director of the Coptic Museum at Cairo. He published reproductions of photographs of another volume in the collection. This volume contains not only a version of the Gnostic Apocryphon of John (a document which in a different form was known to Church writers as early as the second century), but also two "gospels," one ascribed to the apostle Philip, the other to the apostle Thomas. The Apocryphon of John is a Gnostic account of the origin of the universe and of human history. The Gospel of Philip contains nothing but Gnostic speculations.

The Gospel of Thomas, on the other hand, lies close to early Christianity. Its esoteric nature makes it different from the canonical gospels, and the point of view it represents is one which the Church rejected. Fascinating problems remain, however. To what extent is Thomas based on our gospels? Where it is different from them? Why is it different? How was it put together, and what kind of religion does it represent? Questions like these demand answers.

The Gospel of Thomas is the most important document discovered at Nag Hammadi. Compared with it, the other books (except perhaps for the Gospel of Truth) shed little direct light on early Christianity, even though they illuminate the Gnostic religion, which was a rival of Christianity. The Gospel of Thomas shows how Gnostics understood, or rather, misunderstood, Jesus and his gospel. It shows how they constructed a bridge between their own faith and that of the Christian Church. It is probably our most significant witness to the early perversion of Christianity by those who wanted to create Jesus in their own image. Thus it stands, like Lot's wife, as a new but permanently valuable witness to men's desire to make God's revelation serve them. Ultimately it testifies not to what Jesus said but to what men wished he had said.

II

GOSPELS

Everyone knows that for nearly two thousand years the Christian Church has had four gospels, traditionally ascribed to two apostles, Matthew and John, and to two disciples of apostles, Mark and Luke. Not everyone remembers that these gospels were selected by the Church out of a larger number of books which were in circulation from at least the second century onward. During the second and third centuries the leaders of the Church decided that the four gospels were "canonical"; this is to say, they belonged to a "canon," a list of books approved for public reading in the Church's worship. The gospels which were rejected were called "bastard" or "apocryphal." They were not legitimate, and they were used only by minority groups which kept them secret.

The several gospels gave various accounts of the life and teaching of Jesus; the apocryphal gospels differed from the canonical ones in that the portraits of Jesus they presented were usually in harmony with the doctrines of some sect rather than with those of the Church as a whole. The problem thus presented is not simply an ancient one. Similar difficulties have arisen in modern times, when scholars representing various viewpoints have composed remarkably different "lives of Jesus." The disagreements, as we shall see, are due not simply to differing ideas about historical evidence but also to the theological presuppositions which are involved. Both factors are important.

We shall consider, first, the variety present within the four gospels; second, the continuing use of oral tradition (on which the other gospels were often said to be based); and, finally, the remains of the apocryphal gospels themselves.

A. THE TESTIMONY OF THE GOSPELS

One of the most difficult problems which the Christian Church confronted in its early years was presented by the existence of various accounts of the life and teaching of Jesus. This problem had arisen well before the end of the first century; two of the evangelists allude to it—Luke, at the beginning of his gospel, John, at the end of his. Luke speaks of the "many" writers who had undertaken to compose a narrative about the events which had taken place among Christians; he insists that his own version is reliable because it is based on careful analysis of accounts transmitted by eyewitnesses. John states that Jesus effected many miraculous signs not recorded in "this book," but he indicates what his own principle of selection was. "These have been written so that you may believe that Jesus is the Christ, the Son of God, and so that by believing you may have life in his name."

The two principles the evangelists mention are permanently significant. The first is that of historical reliability. Jesus was a real person, who lived, died, and rose from the dead in first-century Palestine. He was really born; he really proclaimed his gospel to human beings in a historical setting; his gospel consists partly of what he actually did and partly of what he actually said. The Christian religion is based, in part, on the genuine, historical deeds and words of Jesus.

Luke is not the only early Christian who insisted on this point. The apostle Paul also emphasized the importance of the "happenedness" of the tradition. "If Christ was not raised, our proclamation is in vain and our faith is in vain, and we are found to be bearing false witness against God" (1 Corinthians 15:14–15). Paul's vision of reality depended on the historical truthfulness of the resurrection tradition. Similarly, the First Epistle of John opens with the words: "That which was from the beginning, which we heard, which we beheld with our eyes, which we saw and our hands handled . . . we beheld and we testify." These words mean that faith and fact, in the minds of early Christian writers, could not be divorced. Theological significance was not something which could be distilled out of historical events and preserved by itself. Early Christians did not use the word "myth" in a refined, Platonic sense. On the contrary, they rejected the notion that myths were in any way related to their gospel. "It was not by following cleverly devised myths that we made known to you the power and presence of our Lord Jesus Christ," says the author of 2 Peter (1:16).

The second principle was just as important as the first. The earliest Christians were not reporting historical facts because they were historians. They were concerned with what the facts meant for their faith. Indeed, the facts were reported for no other reason than that they produced belief "that Jesus is the Christ," since this belief was the ground of the Christian hope for life in the new age, in the kingdom of God. Jesus was not a "mere man" or a "man among men"; he was the Son of Man and the Son of God who had come to proclaim his Father's reign and to inaugurate it. To have faith in Jesus meant to follow him and to obey him. It meant that the believer would, and already did, participate in the life and action of God.

Both historical reliability and theological significance, then, were important in the minds of the evangelists and of other Christians in the first century. When the words of Jesus, and the stories about his deeds, were first handed down by word of mouth, Christians tried to preserve accuracy while insisting on relevance. We can see this double concern reflected in a letter which the apostle Paul wrote to the Corinthians in about A.D. 53. He was setting forth rules for them to follow in regard to marriage and divorce, and he carefully stated that, for married persons, he was repeating what the Lord had said: "A wife is not to be separated from her husband . . . and a husband is not to leave his wife" (1 Corinthians 7:10–11). Further problems arising from "mixed marriages" of Christians with non-Christians are solved by Paul himself, and he makes very clear the fact that it is he who is solving them, "not the Lord" (7:12). Similarly, when he is dealing with the lives of unmarried persons he says, "I do not have a command of the Lord, but I give a judgment as a man mercifully permitted by the Lord to be trustworthy" (7:25). These verses clearly show that the authority of the words of Jesus was binding upon Paul and upon his congregration. They also show that Paul was extremely careful to indicate the points at which he was going beyond the words of Jesus. We cannot tell whether the Corinthian Christians did or did not have written collections of Jesus's words, though it is at least possible that both Paul and his converts possessed such documents.

The tradition, whether oral or written, was so significant that Paul could rebuke the Corinthians for their unseemly behavior at worship by referring to what Jesus did and said at his Last Supper (1 Corinthians 11:23–25). He says that he received this tradition "from the Lord"—

presumably the Lord as known in the tradition of the Church. The tradition also included a list of the resurrection appearances of Jesus to his disciples (15:3–7), and Paul could appeal to the Lord's command to evangelists that they should "make their living from the gospel" (9:14).

It is evident that behind Paul's letters there lies a collection, or a group of collections, of reports of the deeds and the sayings of Jesus. Such collections lie at the core of our gospels. The Gospel of Mark, for example, has been described as an "extended passion narrative." This phrase means that the real heart of Mark is its account of Jesus's last days in Jerusalem, to which the first thirteen chapters of the book serve as an introduction. All four of our gospels agree, generally, in their reports of Jesus's trial and crucifixion. Paul himself alludes to a narrative in which it must have been reported; for he speaks of the Last Supper as taking place "in the night in which he [Jesus] was betrayed" (1 Corinthians 11:23). This story of Christ's crucifixion, and of the events leading up to it, was preserved because it was important both historically and theologically. In addition, however, there was some outline of his earlier ministry, and there were collections of his sayings, preserved because they gave guidance for living or described the meaning of that reign of God which he had already begun to effect.

Collections of the sayings underlie all four of our gospels. For instance, in Mark 2:1–3:6, there is a collection of sayings and of deeds related to controversies with the Pharisees and other opponents of Jesus; in Mark 4 there is a collection of parables; in Mark 9:33–50 there is a group of sayings arranged largely by verbal association; and in Mark 13 there are sayings about the signs of the end of the age. In Matthew 5–7 we find the "Sermon on the Mount," a collection of sayings assembled partly by subjects and partly by verbal association. Luke has provided an arrangement of his own (9:51–18:14); he sets sayings of various kinds in the context of Jesus's journey toward Jerusalem.

We cannot tell whether these collections were made by the evangelists or by their predecessors. In any event, their existence is obvious, and so is the fact that they produce rather different impressions of the teaching of Jesus. Further divergent impressions result from some of the attitudes toward Jesus which the evangelists emphasize. For example, Matthew is more anxious than the others are to show that Jesus fulfilled Old Testament prophecy; he is also more anxious to present Jesus's teaching as a new law, based upon that of Moses but going beyond it. Luke emphasizes the free grace and forgiveness of God in a group of parables given in chapters 15 and 16. Matthew is concerned with the mission to Jews; Luke, with that to gentiles. In spite of the differences, however, the portrait of Jesus which the three "synoptic" gospels (Matthew, Mark, Luke) present is relatively uniform. In part, the agreement is due to the fact that, at least in their present form, both Matthew and Luke make use of Mark. His outline of Jesus's ministry is, in general, theirs.

The situation is somewhat different when we turn to the Gospel of John. Where the synoptic gospels agree that Jesus's ministry was centered first in Galilee and only afterward in Jerusalem, John tells us that he moved back and forth from Galilee to Jerusalem. According to the synoptic outline, the cleansing of the temple took place toward the end of Jesus's mission; in John it is placed near the beginning. According to the synoptics, Jesus was crucified on the day after the Passover; according to John, he was crucified just before the Passover. The sayings of Jesus in the Fourth Gospel are different from those in the synoptics, both in form and in content. In the synoptics

Jesus speaks much in parables and in short, pointed sayings; in John he gives extended discourses on his relation
to the Father and on the disciples' relation to both the
Son and the Father. In the synoptics the center of his
message lies in the kingdom of God; in John the center is
Jesus himself. The synoptics place Jesus in a setting where
we hear of people possessed by demons and of his miraculous expulsion of demons; where we hear of repentance
and the forgiveness of sins; where we hear of prayer, fasting, and almsgiving. All these features are lacking in John,
but they are found in writings which reflect the popular
Judaism of the first century. Similarly, the synoptics often
quote or allude to the Old Testament, while in John such
quotations, at least, are much less frequent.

Yet John insists on the historical reliability of his gospel.
When he describes the Crucifixion, he tells us that "he
who beheld has borne witness, and his testimony is true,
and he knows that he speaks truly, so that you also may
believe" (19:35). The testimony is true, and it has theological significance, for it results in faith. What are we to
make of the differences between John and the synoptics,
in the light of this statement?

First we should say that the problem is not new. As
early as the second century, Christian writers were aware
that the four gospels differ. Indeed, a small group called
the Alogi argued that because the events described in the
opening chapters of John disagree so much with those in
the synoptics, John's gospel ought to be rejected by the
Church. A Christian apologist named Tatian, on the other
hand, took the four gospels and combined them in his
Diatessaron; he retained the order of none of them, though
for the Galilean ministry of Jesus he relied primarily on
Matthew, and, for the story of the Crucifixion, on John.
At Alexandria the Christian scholars Clement and Origen
held that the synoptics provided a literal, historical account

of Jesus's work, while John composed an allegorical version which gave the inward, spiritual meaning of Jesus. Origen sometimes argued that all four gospels were partly historical and partly symbolical.

Our own conclusions are rather like those of the last writers we have mentioned. All four gospels start from the traditions which their authors knew. The evangelists had no reason to suppose that what they wrote was not historically reliable. But each evangelist, writing with the theological situation of his church in mind, had a slightly different purpose as he wrote. Because the situation of his church corresponded almost exactly with his own theological intention, his gospel was regarded as authoritative. Because in each case the gospel set forth the common faith not of one community but of many communities, it came to be accepted by all. Perhaps it is so that the synoptic gospels are closer to the common Christianity of the first and early second centuries, and also closer to "the historical Jesus." Certainly the sayings they contain are often reflected in Christian literature of the early period, while those set forth by John are less frequently cited. But at a very early time the Church found that its faith was adequately stated not in the synoptic gospels alone, or in any one of them, but in the four gospels. In the letters of Ignatius, bishop of Antioch about 115, we find clear reflections of sayings of Jesus both synoptic and Johannine. The living, growing faith of the Church required both forms of expression. The Jesus whom the Church remembered was the person described both in the synoptic gospels and in John. He was a person who transcended the bounds of history, though he had become incarnate in history. The Church found that he was adequately represented only by three gospels which were relatively more historical (the synoptics) and by one which was relatively more theological (John). By preserving both kinds of testimony, justice could be done both to historical reliability and to theological significance.

B. THE SURVIVAL OF ORAL TRADITION

Though the four gospels had been written and were in circulation long before the end of the first century, Christians continued to make use of oral traditions which told of the life and teaching of Jesus. When Luke wrote the Book of Acts he included in it a saying of Jesus which he had not reported in his gospel: "It is more blessed to give than to receive" (Acts 20:35). In Christian writings of the early second century there are a good many sayings of Jesus which seem to be derived not from written gospels but from oral tradition. And we possess the testimony of a certain Papias, bishop of Hierapolis in Asia Minor, early in the second century, to the survival of oral tradition. Papias certainly knew our Gospel of Mark, probably a version of Matthew, and possibly Luke and John. But he was an assiduous collector of oral tradition. "I supposed," he wrote, "that materials derived from 'the books' did not help me as much as those from a living and continuing voice." On the ground of this belief he asked visitors to Hierapolis for what they knew of the tradition. If they had been followers of any of the disciples of Jesus—such as Andrew, Peter, Philip, Thomas, James, John, or Matthew— he would ask them what their masters had said.

According to the fourth-century historian Eusebius, who preserved most of what we know of Papias' work (now lost), the results were not entirely satisfactory. The daughters of the "apostle" Philip ("evangelist" in Acts 21:9) lived at Hierapolis and told Papias about the resurrection of a dead man; perhaps they also told him about how Justus Barsabbas (Acts 1:23) drank a deadly poison without ill effect. Papias also related "certain strange parables of the

Savior and teachings of his, and some other things of a rather mythical character." What Eusebius meant by his criticism of the sayings of Jesus as transmitted by Papias was that Papias was fond of sayings which spoke of the establishment of the kingdom of God on earth. "He did not understand what they [the apostles] said mystically and in figurative language." More probably what Papias did was to report sayings which reflected the ordinary Jewish Christianity of the first and second centuries. Eusebius found them unpalatable. They were not necessarily false.

On the other hand, our confidence in Papias is not increased when we read a fragment which he says came to him from John, the Lord's disciple. It describes the miraculous fertility of grapevines in the future kingdom. Each vine will produce grapes to the number of ten thousand to the fifth power; each grape will produce "twenty-five measures of wine." Since a similar picture is drawn in a second-century Jewish apocalypse (revelation) called 2 Baruch, we may wonder whether Papias was really very careful about the information he collected. We may wonder whether oral tradition, by his time, was not getting rather garbled.

The evidence provided by Papias does not increase our faith in the reliability of what Gnostic teachers of the second century said about their secret traditions. For instance, at Alexandria, Basilides (who flourished about 117–138) said that he had traditions which came from Peter through his "interpreter" Glaucias—otherwise unknown to us. At Rome, Valentinus, a little later, said that he had been taught by Theodas, a disciple of Paul. One might even suppose that these notions were developed in imitation of what the Church said about its own evangelists, for Papias describes Mark as the interpreter of Peter, and according to tradition, Luke was a disciple of Paul.

Glaucias may have been a substitute for Mark; Theodas, for Luke. It is possible, however, that Basilides knew an interpreter of Peter and Valentinus, a disciple of Paul. Both Peter and Paul doubtless had disciples whose grasp of the Christian gospel was imperfect or, indeed, entirely inadequate. The basic point is not whether the "traditions" of Basilides and Valentinus ultimately came from the apostles or not. The point is that their traditions did not correspond with those which the Church included in its portrait of Jesus. The Jesus of the Gnostics is a completely otherworldly figure who did not really live on earth and came only to help men to escape from this life. This is not the person we encounter in any of the four gospels.

C. THE APOCRYPHAL GOSPELS

According to Eusebius, Papias "set forth a story about a woman falsely accused of many sins before the Lord, which the Gospel of the Hebrews contains." This story is probably not the one concerning the woman taken in adultery, inserted in most manuscripts of the New Testament after the late fourth century, but not earlier (usually at John 7:53–8:11), since in the New Testament story the accusation is true. We do not know whether or not Papias derived it from the Gospel of the Hebrews, but the Jewish-Christian atmosphere of his writings suggests that he may well have done so. If he did, this is our earliest testimony to the existence of any of the apocryphal gospels.

These apocryphal gospels gave the Church a great deal of difficulty in the second and third centuries. Though Irenaeus, bishop of Lyons about 180, insisted that there could be only four gospels, minority groups within the Church and outside it continued to make use of other gospels which reflected their own points of view. The

Gospel of the Hebrews, one of the oldest of them, sets forth the faith of Jewish Christians; the Gospel of the Egyptians, that of Christians already moving toward Gnosticism. There were many such gospels in the early days, and most of them have survived only in fragments, because the Church was anxious to suppress them. The many lists of authoritative books produced from the second century onward mention these gospels only in order to reject them.

Most of the fragments of the Gospel of the Hebrews which we possess were copied by Jerome, who wrote in the late fourth and early fifth centuries. We therefore cannot be absolutely certain that this gospel was exactly the same as that which earlier writers mention. Jerome makes no mention of a fragment which is quoted in a Coptic version of a sermon by Cyril of Jerusalem (about 350). Theologically it is extraordinary. The archangel Michael turns into the virgin Mary and bears Christ.[1]

When Christ wished to come upon earth to men, the Good Father summoned a mighty Power in the heavens which was called Michael and committed Christ to its care. And the Power came down into the world, and it was called Mary, and Christ was in her womb for seven months.

The descent of the "Power" looks rather like Luke 1:35: "The Holy Spirit will come upon you, and the power of the Most High will overshadow you." [2] But if this statement was in Hebrews, it is hard to see how its author could reconcile it with his notion that the Holy Spirit was the mother of Jesus.

Much of what we find in the other fragments seems to be based on our gospels and on reflection over theological

---

[1] V. Burch, in *Journal of Theological Studies,* XXI (1919–20), 310–11.
[2] Perhaps the "seven months" comes from the mention of the "sixth month" in Luke 1:26.

problems presented by them. For instance, Jerome records two sections of a story about Jesus's baptism.[3]

Behold, the mother of the Lord and his brothers said to him, "John is baptizing for the remission of sins; let us go and be baptized by him." But he said to them, "What sin have I committed, that I should go and be baptized by him—unless perhaps this very statement that I have made is ignorance?"

This looks like an attempt to explain the problem, difficult for early Christians, as to why the sinless Jesus should have been baptized by John; some of them held that he was baptized in order to purify the water.

It came to pass that, when the Lord had come up from the water, the whole fountain of the Holy Spirit descended and rested upon him [Isaiah 11:2; 61:1] and said to him, "My son, in all the prophets I was waiting for you, so that you would come and I might rest in you. For you are my rest [Psalms 132:14]; you are my first-born son [cf., Psalms 2:7], who will reign forever."

This saying reflects the doctrine of Hebrews that the Spirit was Christ's mother. Otherwise it is simply a rewriting of the synoptic story of his baptism.

Immediately after Jesus's baptism must be placed the saying which was known not only to Jerome but also, earlier, to Origen.[4]

"Then my mother the Holy Spirit took me by one of my hairs and brought me to the great mount Tabor."

This saying is intended to contradict the gospel story that it was the devil who took Jesus away for his temptation; it is based on Old Testament stories about the work of the Spirit in lifting men up, such as Ezekiel 8:3 ("He

---

[3] *Dial. adv. Pelag.*, 3, 2 (Migne, PL 23, 570); *Comm. in Is.* 11, 2 (PL 24, 144–45).
[4] Origen, *Comm. in Joh.*, 2, 12, etc.

took me by a lock of my head, and the Spirit lifted me up between earth and heaven") or Bel and the Dragon 36 ("Then the angel of the Lord lifted him by his hair and set him down in Babylon"). Clearly secondary, the saying ascribed to Jesus is vivid but not therefore authentic.

Eusebius, as we have seen, tells us that this gospel contained a story of a woman "accused of many sins before the Lord," [5] and it may be that this story was that now usually printed in English versions of the New Testament as John 7:53–8:11. More probably, however, it was a variation on the same theme; the story in John describes her as accused of only one sin. Other stories in Hebrews are variants of gospel materials. Instead of one rich man, as in Matthew 19:16–26, Hebrews has two.[6] In the Hebrews version of the parable of the talents (Matthew 25:14–30) there are three slaves, but one of them uses up his master's property with harlots and flute girls (and is put in prison), another buries the talent (and is criticized), and the third multiplies it (and is accepted by his master).[7] To the verses in which Peter is told to forgive "seventy times seven" (Matthew 18:21–22), Hebrews adds a saying of Jesus: "For also in the prophets, after they were anointed by the Holy Spirit, there was found a matter of sin." [8]

Other sayings of Jesus, or rather sayings ascribed to Jesus, found in this gospel are as follows: [9]

I choose for myself the best that my Father who is in heaven gives me.
You will never be glad until you look upon your brother with love.
Give us today our bread of tomorrow.

[5] H. E., 3, 39, 17.
[6] Pseudo-Origen (PL 13, 1393–94).
[7] Eusebius, On the Theophany (PG 24, 685–86).
[8] Jerome, Dial. adv. Pelag., 3, 2 (PL 23, 570).
[9] Eusebius, On the Theophany, 4, 12; Jerome, Comm. in Eph., 5, 4 (PL 26, 520); Comm. in Matt., 6, 11 (PL 26, 43).

All these look like attempts to interpret earlier gospel writings. The first seems to be a combination of Matthew 7:21 with John 17:6. The second adds little to what we find in the authentic sayings of Jesus. The third seems to be an explanation of the difficult Greek word *epiousios*, found in that part of the Lord's Prayer in Matthew 6:11. It may be the correct explanation, but this possibility does not prove that Hebrews used authentic, original sources.

Finally, the author of Hebrews gives us some interesting alternative versions of the story of Christ's crucifixion and resurrection. Where the synoptic evangelists state that the veil of the temple was rent at the Crucifixion, this author apparently believes that Isaiah 6:4 contains a prophecy which must be fulfilled and therefore says that the threshold stone in the temple broke.[10] And the concern of this gospel for Jewish-Christian tradition and authority is reflected in its story of the resurrection. Here it is James, the Lord's brother, bishop of Jerusalem, who is the earliest witness—not Peter.

But the Lord, when he had given the linen garment to the high priest's slave, went to James and appeared to him; for James had sworn that he would not eat bread from that hour when he had drunk the Lord's cup until he saw him rising from those who sleep. . . . "Bring," says the Lord, "a table and bread." He took bread and blessed it and broke it and gave it to James the Just and said to him, "My brother, eat your bread, for the Son of Man has arisen from those who sleep." [11]

In this story the author of Hebrews has managed to include several highly biased notions. First, he has made James the Just (a second-century title for the Lord's brother) a guest at the Last Supper. Second, he has made James take an oath there like that which Jesus himself

[10] Jerome, *Comm. in Matt.*, 27, 51 (PL 26, 213).
[11] Jerome, *De viris inlustr.*, 2.

35

took. Third, he has introduced the "high priest's slave" of John 18:10 into the resurrection story, though his reason for doing so is not clear. Fourth, Jesus appears in a Eucharistic setting strongly reminiscent of Luke 24:30, though James, not Cleopas and another, is the witness to it. In general, the sole purpose of this story is to strengthen the claims of the Church of Jerusalem at the expense of gentile Christians.

Gentile Christians, or rather, their spiritual founder Peter and his companions, are mentioned in another fragment.[12]

And when he came to Peter and to those who were with Peter, he said to them, "Behold, handle me and see [Luke 24:39] that I am not an incorporeal demon."

Ignatius of Antioch, our oldest witness to the existence of this saying, does not state that it comes from a gospel writing, and it is quite possible that in his version it is based on memories of Luke 24:39. On the other hand, Jerome definitely says that it is found in Hebrews. We should assume either that Jerome's memory failed him (Origen says the saying was found in the Teaching of Peter) or that the author of Hebrews had heard the saying in the form given it by Ignatius. A definite decision is hard to reach, but in any event the expression "incorporeal demon" is not likely to be primitive. It has philosophical overtones which are absent from the early traditions.

Toward the end of the second century Alexandrian and Roman writers report the existence of another apocryphal gospel which seems to have been especially important. This is the Gospel according to the Egyptians, used by Gnostic groups and perhaps by the author of 2 Clement, a Roman writer of the mid-second century.

---

[12] *Ibid.*, 16; cf., Ignatius, *Smyrn.*, 3, 2.

The Gospel according to the Egyptians was written by someone who was on his way toward Gnosticism, whether he reached his destination or not. It contains a dialogue between Jesus and one of his disciples about the time when his kingdom, or "the end," would come. In 2 Clement (12:2) the answer is given thus: "When the two are one, and the outside like the inside, and the male with the female neither male nor female." Clement of Alexandria reproduces the dialogue more fully,[13] ascribing part of it to Salome, otherwise unknown.[14]

Salome said, "How long will men die?"
The Lord replied, "As long as you women bring forth."
Salome replied, "I did well, then, by not bringing forth."
The Lord said, "Eat every plant, but do not eat the one which contains bitterness [cf., Gen. 3:16]."
Salome asked when what she was inquiring about would be known.
The Lord said, "When you trample on the garment of shame, and when the two become one, and the male with the female neither male nor female."

Elsewhere Clement reports a saying from the gospel which seems to be related to this conversation.[15]

The Savior himself said, "I came to destroy the works of the female."

This reminds us of the "programmatic" sayings in the synoptic gospels, but the content is, of course, entirely different. The saying represents the thoroughgoing ascetic attitude to be found in the Docetic-Gnostic "traditions."

Other testimonies given by anti-heretical writers show that there was further theological analysis in this gospel. Hippolytus tells us that the Naassene Gnostics found their

[13] *Stromata*, 3, 64, 1 (3, 45, 3); 3, 66, 1-2; 3, 92, 2.
[14] Perhaps regarded as a woman who came with Jesus from Galilee to Jerusalem (Mark 15:40).
[15] *Strom.*, 3, 63, 1-2.

doctrine of the mutability of the soul expressed in Egyptians, and according to Epiphanius, it contained the Sabellian teaching, ascribed to the Savior, that Father, Son, and Holy Spirit are identical.[16]

Obviously, when we look at these fragments we can see that the Church was right when either on historical or theological grounds it rejected the book. It is a witness to the freely creative imagination of those who handed down and compiled Gnostic or semi-Gnostic "traditions." They wanted to "destroy the works of the female," but related conversations of Jesus with women. Some sort of ambivalence seems to be indicated here.

We have seen that, toward the end of the second century, Clement of Alexandria mentioned and quoted both the Gospel according to the Hebrews and the Gospel according to the Egyptians. These, of course, were not the only apocryphal gospels there were. Serapion, bishop of Antioch around Clement's time, was able to examine the apocryphal Gospel of Peter, and to critize its contents. A few years earlier, Irenaeus knew of the Gospel of Truth, which the Valentinian Gnostics used. And Clement's successor at Alexandria, the famous Origen, speaks of apocryphal gospels in his first homily on Luke. Among the gospels rejected, says Origen, were the Gospel according to the Egyptians, the Gospel of the Twelve (otherwise unknown), and the Gospel according to Thomas. Origen's contemporary Hippolytus gives a quotation from the Gospel of Thomas, which, he says, was used by the Gnostic group called Naassenes.[17]

He who seeks me will find me in children over seven years old; for there, in the fourteenth age, though hidden I shall be manifest.

---

[16] Hippolytus, *Ref.*, 5, 7, 9; Epiphanius, *Pan.*, 62, 2, 4.
[17] *Op. cit.*, 5, 7, 20.

The sense of this fragment is not self-evident, and the meaning of the Gospel of Thomas as a whole could not be recovered from it. Not until the recent discovery of the Coptic Thomas was evidence available for the study of this gospel. And Thomas is especially significant because it is the only complete early apocryphal gospel which we possess.

III

GOSPEL FINDINGS
IN THE PAPYRI

Until the end of the nineteenth century the only gospels
or collections of sayings of Jesus which were known were
the four canonical gospels and the fragments discussed
in the last chapter. During the winter of 1886–1887, however, a French archaeological expedition was digging in
Christian graves at Akhmim in Upper Egypt when its
members found a small bound volume containing thirty-
three parchment leaves from the eighth or ninth century.[1]
On these leaves were written Greek fragments of the
Gospel and Apocalypse of Peter, as well as of the Jewish-
Christian book of Enoch.

A. THE GOSPEL OF PETER

Scholars had long known of the existence of the Gospel
of Peter, for it had been mentioned—and rejected—by
Origen in the third century and Eusebius in the fourth.
Indeed, Eusebius reproduced part of a letter, written in
about 190 by Serapion of Antioch, in which this gospel was

[1] C. Maurer, in W. Schneemelcher–E. Hennecke, *Neutestamentliche
Apokryphen in deutscher Übersetzung*, I (Tübingen, 1959), 118.

criticized. Some Christians in the village of Rhossus, near Antioch, had complained to Serapion about the reading of the Gospel of Peter; Serapion had rejected their complaint, after glancing at the book. Later he obtained a copy from heretics who favored "Docetism"—the doctrine that Jesus merely seemed to suffer but, as a divine being, did not really do so—and looked through it more carefully. He found that, while the book was largely harmless there were passages in it which favored heresy. He thereupon sent a list of such passages (which Eusebius did not copy) to Rhossus.[2]

The mixture which Serapion discovered is exactly what we have in the Akhmim fragment, which we now translate.

(1) But none of the Jews washed his hands, nor did Herod or any of his judges; and when they did not want to wash, Pilate stood up. And then King Herod ordered the Lord to be delivered, saying to them, "What I have ordered you to do to him, do it."

(2) Joseph, the friend of Pilate and of the Lord, stood there, and knowing that they were going to crucify him, he came to Pilate and asked for the Lord's body for burial. And Pilate sent to Herod and asked him for the body, and Herod said, "Brother Pilate, had no one asked for him we should bury him, since a Sabbath is dawning; for it is written in the law that the sun does not set upon a murdered man."

(3) And he delivered him to the people before the first day of unleavened bread, their feast. They took the Lord and pushed him as they ran, and said, "Let us greet the Son of God, since we have authority over him." And they clad him in purple and seated him on a judgment seat, saying, "Judge justly, King of Israel." And someone brought him a crown of thorns and put it on the Lord's head; and others standing by spat on his eyes and others smote his cheeks. Others pierced him with a reed, and some beat him, saying, "With this honor let us honor the Son of God."

[2] Eusebius, *H. E.*, 6, 12.

(4) And they brought two malefactors, and they crucified the Lord between them; but he was silent, since he felt no pain. And when they had set up the cross, they wrote on it, "This is the King of Israel." And they laid their garments before it and cast lots upon them. One of those malefactors cursed them, saying, "We have suffered thus because of the wrongs we committed; but this one, who has become Savior of men, what harm has he done you?" And being indignant against him, they ordered that his legs should not be broken, that he might die in torment.

(5) It was noon, and darkness came over all Judea; and they were troubled and distressed for fear that the sun had set, since he was still alive; for it is written for them that the sun should not set on a murdered man. And one of them said, "Give him a drink of gall with vinegar"; and they mixed it and gave him to drink. And they fulfilled everything, and they completed their sins against their head. Many went about with lamps, supposing that it was night, [and some] fell down. And the Lord cried out, saying, "My power, my power, you have left me." And when he spoke he was taken up. And at that very hour the veil of the temple in Jerusalem was torn in two.

(6) And then they drew the nails from the Lord's hands and they put him on the ground, and the whole earth was shaken and there was great fear. Then the sun shone and it was found to be the ninth hour. The Jews rejoiced and gave Joseph his body so that he might bury it, since he had witnessed all the good deeds which he (the Lord) had done. Taking the Lord, he washed him and wrapped him in linen and brought him to his own tomb, called Joseph's Garden.

(7) Then the Jews and the elders and the priests, knowing what evil they had done to themselves, began to lament and to say, "Woe to our sins; the judgment and the end of Jerusalem is at hand." I (Peter) with my companions was grieving, and being wounded in mind we hid ourselves; for we were being sought by them as malefactors and as men who wished to burn the temple; and in addition to all this, we were fasting, and we sat mourning and weeping night and day until the Sabbath.

(8) The scribes and Pharisees and elders met together,

having heard that the whole people was murmuring and beating their breasts and saying, "If these very great signs took place at his death, see how righteous he was." The elders were afraid, and they came to Pilate, asking him and saying, "Give us soldiers, so that we may guard his sepulcher for three days, lest his disciples come and steal him, and the people suppose that he has risen from the dead and do us harm." Pilate gave them Petronius the centurion, with soldiers, to guard the tomb. And with them elders and scribes came to the sepulcher, and having rolled a great stone to exclude the centurion and the soldiers, all who were there together placed it against the door of the sepulcher, and they sealed it with seven seals, and pitched a tent there and kept guard. In the morning, when the Sabbath had dawned, a crowd came from Jerusalem and the surrounding country to see the sealed sepulcher.

(9) In the night when the Lord's Day was dawning, and the soldiers were on guard two by two in a watch, there was a great voice in heaven, and they saw the heavens opened and two men who came down from there and had a great light and drew near the tomb. And that stone which had been cast at the door rolled away of its own accord and made way in part, and the tomb was opened, and both the young men entered. When those soldiers saw this, they awakened the centurion and the elders (for they too were there on guard); and while they were recounting what they had seen, again they see three men coming out of the tomb, and the two supporting the one, and a cross following them, and the head of the two reaching to heaven, and that of the one conducted by them surpassing the heavens. And they heard a voice from the heavens saying, "Have you preached to those who sleep?" And a response was heard from the cross: "Yes."

(10) They took counsel, therefore, with one another to go and report these things to Pilate. And while they were still considering it, the heavens appeared opened again, and a man descended and entered the sepulcher. Having seen this, those about the centurion hastened at night to Pilate, leaving the tomb which they were guarding, and they recounted every-

thing they had seen, greatly distressed and saying, "Truly he was the Son of God." Pilate answered and said, "I am clean of the blood of the Son of God; this seemed good to you." Then they all came and asked him to order the centurion and the soldiers to say nothing of what they had seen. For, "It is expedient for us," they said, "to be guilty of a very great sin before God, and not to fall into the hands of the people of the Jews and be stoned." Then Pilate ordered the centurion and the soldiers to say nothing.

(11) At dawn on the Lord's Day, Mariam Magdalene, the Lord's disciple (afraid because of the Jews, since they were inflamed with wrath, she had not done at the Lord's sepulcher what women are accustomed to do for the dead and for those who love them), took with her her friends and came to the sepulcher where he had been laid. And they were afraid that the Jews would see them, and they said, "If we could not weep and mourn for him on that day when he was crucified, yet now let us do so at his sepulcher. Who will roll away for us the stone which was laid at the door of the sepulcher, so that we may go in and sit by him and do what is suitable? For the stone was great, and we are afraid that someone may see us. And if we cannot, even if we cast at the door the things which we bring in remembrance of him, we will weep and mourn for him until we come to our house." And they went and found the tomb opened, and they came near and stooped down there, and they see a young man there, sitting in the midst of the tomb, beautiful and clad with a very bright robe, who said to them, "Why have you come? Whom do you seek? Is it that crucified one? He has risen and has gone away. If you do not believe, stoop down and see the place where he lay, that he is not here; for he is risen and has gone to the place from which he was sent." Then the women were afraid and fled.

(12) It was the last day of unleavened bread, and many went out of the city, returning to their houses, since the feast had ended. But we, the twelve disciples of the Lord, were weeping and grieving, and each one, grieving for what had happened, withdrew to his house. But I, Simon Peter, and

Andrew my brother, took our nets and went away to the sea; and with us there was Levi, son of Alphaeus, whom the Lord . . .

This Gospel of Peter has been studied intensively by many scholars, and their results confirm the opinion of it expressed by Serapion. In many respects it is like the four canonical gospels; indeed, it includes every incident in the story of Christ's crucifixion which is told in all four, though its author seems to avoid the precise wording found in them. This avoidance is doubtless due to his fictitious claim to be Simon Peter.

On the other hand, there are some significant additions. Perhaps the most important are these: (1) the increased emphasis given Herod's role; (2) Christ's freedom from pain as explaining his silence; (3) his cry, "My power, my power, you have forsaken me"; (4) details about the burial, with mention of the centurion Petronius and seven seals on the tomb; (5) a fabulous story of Christ's resurrection; (6) strange new stories about the empty tomb and later events.

From these points, some of the purposes of "Peter" can be determined. The first point, as well as many minor details, is intended to make the Jews responsible for the crucifixion and to relieve Pilate of any blame. This notion seems to have become more prominent after the first century. The second, third, and fifth points represent attempts to explain Christ's divine nature (though in a rather peculiar way) at the expense of his humanity. The fourth and sixth points can be interpreted as reflections of the love of storytelling for its own sake which is characteristic of apocryphal literature generally.

There is no reason to suppose that Peter contains any authentic traditions at all; indeed, one saying in it (section 7), "Woe to our sins; the judgment and the end of

Jerusalem is at hand," is very similar to a late interpolation which we find in a few manuscripts of the Gospel of Luke (23:48: "Woe to us, the things which were done today because of our sins; for the desolation of Jerusalem is at hand."). If "Peter" derived his statement from this late version of Luke, as we may suspect he did, his gospel must surely be placed quite late in the second century. In any case, it is absolutely worthless for trying to recover genuine materials concerning the words or deeds of Jesus. The one saying of Jesus it contains ("My power, my power, you have forsaken me") is a forced revision, or a mistranslation, of the genuine word, "My God, my God, why have you forsaken me?" (Mark 15:34 and parallels.) [3]

Our reason for translating it and discussing it is to provide some orientation in regard to the modern discoveries which have often been loudly acclaimed at first and then gradually relegated to the area in which they belong. This area is not the life of Jesus or the authentic tradition of his sayings; it is the borderline between Christianity and its offshoots which existed in the second century and later. In other words, Peter and similar documents are more significant for the study of early Christian literature than of the New Testament, of early Church history than of the life of Jesus.

These documents possess value only in so far as they remind us of two facts. First, they provide us with materials with which to compare the canonical gospels, even though in nearly every instance the comparison proves that the canonical gospels are more original. Second, they continue to pose the question rightly raised by historical critics in regard to the authenticity of the materials found within as well as outside the canon. Even if we conclude that all apocryphal materials are more or less fictitious, we still

---

[3] It may be that the author, like first-century Jews, is avoiding the word "God."

must try to assess the genuineness of what is not apocryphal. If the Christian religion is based on historical revelation, the record of the revelation must be examined historically.

B. THE OXYRHYNCHUS PAPYRI

Further stimulus was given the study of non-canonical sayings of Jesus in 1897, when the first volume of papyri found at Oxyrhynchus in Egypt was published. The very first of these papyri, a fragment from the third century of our era, contained seven sayings of Jesus in a good state of preservation, though the first of them evidently began in the middle. These were the sayings:

1

and then you will see
to cast out the mote
which is in the eye
of your brother.

2

Says
Jesus: unless you fast
to the world, you will not
find the kingdom
of God, and unless
you "sabbatize" the Sab-
bath, you will not see the
Father.

3

Says Jesus: I stood
in the midst of the world
and I appeared in flesh
to them and I found all
drunken and
I found none thirs-

ty among them. And my
soul grieves over
the sons of men,
for they are blind in
their heart and they do not
see . . .

. . . poverty . . .

4

Says Jesus: where there are
[two, they are not] without God, and
where there is one alone,
[I say], I am with him.
Lift the stone,
and there you will find me;
split the wood, and I
am there.

5

Says Jesus: no
prophet is acceptable
in his native country,
nor does a physician work
cures on those
who know him.

6

Says Jesus: a city built
on the summit
of a high mountain and
fortified cannot
fall nor
be concealed.

7

Says Jesus: You
hear in one ear what

. . .

48

A few years later, in 1903, two different fragments were found at Oxyrhynchus. They seemed to come from the same collection of sayings of Jesus, and one of them actually contained the beginning of such a collection. Unfortunately they were in much worse condition than the first find had been.

The first papyrus (P. Oxy. IV, 654) read as follows:

1

These are the words which [. . .
spoke Jesus the living L [ord . . .
and to Thomas, and he said [. . . whoever [hears] these words [. . . death
he will not taste.

2

[Says Jesus:
let him who seeks not cease [. . . until
he finds, and when he finds [he will marvel
and when he marvels he will reign [and when he reigns
he will rest.

The third and fourth sayings were remarkably difficult to reconstruct, and different scholars inevitably supplied different supplements. The text was as follows:

3

Says Jesus [. . .
who draw us . . .
the kingdom in heaven . . .
the birds of the heaven . . .
what under the earth . . .
the fishes of the sea . . .
. . you, and the kingdom . . .
is within you . . .
know, will find it . . .
to know yourselves . . .
you are of the Father who . . .

49

you know yourselves in . . .
and you are the . . .

4
a man will not hesitate
to ask . . .
. . about the place of . . .
you, that many will be f . . .
and the last, first, and . . .
will.

Some of the words could easily be restored; thus in the fourth line of the fourth saying an obvious restoration was "many will be first [who are] last" (Greek word order permits this). To restore the rest was more difficult.

Fortunately the fifth saying was clearer.

5
Says Jesus: [everything not
before your sight and [what is hidden
from you will be revealed [to you. Nothing
hidden will not manifest [become
and buried which will not [be (raised?)

But the sixth saying becomes more obscure.

6
There ask him [his disciples and
say: How shall we fast [and how
shall we [. . .] and how [. . .
. . . and what shall we observe . . .
. . . Says Jesus: . . .
. . . will be. Do not do . . .
. . . of truth . . .
. . . hidden . . .
. . . blessed is . . .

The rest is too fragmentary to translate, and the whole saying was characterized by the word "hidden" in the eighth line. As we shall later see, the British scholar H. B. Swete was quite right when he restored the first three lines as "How shall we fast and how shall we pray and how shall we give alms?" But his other reconstructions were wrong. There was not enough material to serve as a base for recovering the rest.

The other Oxyrhynchus fragment (P. Oxy. IV, 655) contained sayings which were more like those found in the synoptic gospels and hence were easier to restore. Unfortunately the "fragment" is not in one piece but in eight, only two of which are closely connected.

The pieces which clearly go together read as follows:

(a) from morning until evening
[nor] from evening
[until] morning nor [for
your [food] what you will
eat [nor] for [your] rai-
[ment] what you will
(b) wear. You are much
better than the [li-
lies, which neither card
nor spin . . .
having one gar[ment
why do you . . . in . . .?
Who would add
to your stature?
He himself will give you
your garment.
They say to him,
his disciples,
When will you be
visible to us and when
shall we see you? He says,
When you are stripped and
are not ashamed . . .

(b) They [took the key
of [knowledge and
hid [it; they did not
enter [in, nor to those
entering [did they
[open . . . but you
be [come pru-
dent a[s serpents and sincere [as do-
ves . . .

The only other really legible fragment contains what look like parts of the Greek words for "luminous" and for "world." Scholars could not possibly have reconstructed it, even though the last four lines of the second column of fragment "b" were restored by Charles Taylor from sixteen scattered Greek letters.[4]

Few scholars had any idea of the nature of what had been found. Though the great textual critic Kirsopp Lake restored the words "to Judas who is also Thomas" in the preface to the sayings, few agreed with him. Most scholars were content to analyze the content and authenticity of the sayings, without much success.

In 1905, much to the surprise of scholars, another fragment was found at Oxyrhynchus, containing more sayings of Jesus; this time the sayings were in a context like that found in the canonical gospels. The papyrus (P. Oxy. V, 840) dates from about the year 400. It was published in 1907.

. . . and he took them with him into the very place of purity [*hagneutērion*] and walked in the temple. And a certain Pharisee, a chief priest, Levi by name, came to meet them and said to the Savior,

"Who permitted you to walk upon this place of purity and to look upon these holy vessels, when you have not first washed and your disciples have not washed their feet? But you have walked on this sacred spot in a state of defilement, this clean place, on which no one can walk unless he has washed and has changed his clothes, nor can he venture to look upon these holy vessels."

The Savior stopped with his disciples and answered,

"Since you are in the temple, are you clean?"

---

[4] *The Oxyrhynchus Sayings of Jesus Found in 1903* (Oxford, 1905), 23. We should add that modern discoveries show that "luminous" and "world" come from the Gospel of Thomas, Saying 25. It was Puech who discovered that all three Oxyrhynchus fragments (1, 654, and 655) come from the Gospel of Thomas.

He says to him,

"I am clean; for I have washed in the pool of David and I went down to it by one ladder and up by another, and I have put on clean white clothing, and then I came and looked at these holy vessels."

The Savior answered and said to him,

"Woe to the blind who do not see! You have washed in these waters poured forth, in which dogs and swine lie night and day; and you have washed and scoured your outside skin, which harlots and flute girls anoint and wash and scour and beautify to arouse men's lust, though inwardly it is full of scorpions and all unrighteousness. But I and my [disciples], whom you call unwashed, we have bathed in living waters [. . .] which have come from [. . .] But woe to the . . ."

At this point the papyrus fragment breaks off.

Considerable controversy arose over the authenticity of this dialogue. First, the word we have translated as "chief priest" could also mean "high priest," and there was no high priest named Levi. Second, there is no record that the temple in Jerusalem contained something called a *hagneutērion*, or that there was a "pool of David." Third, the laity were not allowed to inspect the sacred vessels in the temple. In recent times, Joachim Jeremias has countered these objections by insisting on the translation "chief priest" (meaning a temple treasurer or chief of the temple police); he has argued that there could have been both a *hagneutērion* and a pool of David, and that the scene takes place not in the holy place in the temple but in storage chambers surrounding the forecourts.

Yet the arguments of Jeremias do not prove the authenticity of the story. They show only that some of the criticisms made of it are not as conclusive as scholars had thought. Moreover, his arguments are not altogether convincing. The story itself says that Jesus and his disciples were in the "place of purity," "in the temple," not in some area on the outside. And the answer which Jesus makes to Levi clearly seems to be related to the apocryphal Gospel according to the Hebrews. First, there is a mention of "harlots and flute girls," a combination which is found in this gospel.[5] Second, Jesus states that he and his disciples have bathed in living waters. This point implies that they have been baptized, and while we do not have a testimony from Hebrews on this matter, we do know that in the Gospel of the Ebionites the call of the disciples was placed before the baptism of Jesus,[6] presumably so that they too might be baptized.

We may add that the picture of a "pool of David" in which dogs and swine are lying night and day and in which a chief priest bathes remains incredible, in spite of Jeremias' ingenious effort to solve the difficulty by translating a purely hypothetical Aramaic original.[7]

C. AN UNKNOWN GOSPEL

In 1935 two British scholars, H. I. Bell and T. C. Skeat, published some "fragments of an unknown gospel" from a second-century papyrus in the British Museum. This gospel seems to be based chiefly on John and the synoptics, along with some legendary materials.

I

. . . to the lawyers. . . . "Every wrongdoer and [transgressor] and not me . . . how he does . . . and turning to the rulers of the people he spoke this word:

"Search the scriptures; in them you suppose that you have life; they are those which testify about me [John 5:39]. Do not suppose that I came to accuse you before my Father;

[5] Frag. 18 Lagrange.
[6] Frag. 2 Lagrange.
[7] *Unknown Sayings of Jesus* (New York, 1957), 44.

there is one who accuses you, Moses, on whom you have set
your hope [John 5:45]."
But when they said,
"Well we know that God spoke to Moses, but we do not
know you [John 9:29] . . . ,"
Jesus answered and said to them,
"Now your unbelief accuses you . . ." [Cf., John 5:45–47.]

II

. . . to the multitude . . . stones together and stone him
[John 10:31]. The rulers laid their hands on him to take him
and . . . him over to the multitude. And they could not take
him, because the hour of his betrayal had not yet come [John
7:30]. But the Lord himself went out [through their midst]
and departed from [them] [John 10:39; Luke 4:30].
And behold, a leper came to him and says [cf., Matthew 8:2–4;
Mark 1:40–44; Luke 5:12–14],
"Teacher Jesus, when I was traveling with lepers and eating
with them in the inn, I myself became a leper. If you will,
I am cleansed."
Then the Lord said to him,
"I will; be cleansed."
[And immediately] the leprosy departed from him. [The Lord
said to him,]
"Go and [show yourself] to the priests. . . ."

III

Coming to him, they tempted him with a question, saying,
"Teacher Jesus, we know that you have come [from God]
[John 3:2], for what you do testifies above all the prophets.
[Tell us then:] is it lawful [to render] to kings what belongs
to their rule or not?" [cf., Matthew 22:15–22; Mark 12:13–
17; Luke 20:20–26.]
Jesus, knowing their thought, was indignant [Mark 1:43] and
said to them,
"Why do you call me Teacher with your mouth and do not
hear what I say? [cf., Luke 6:46.] Well did Isaiah prophesy
concerning you when he said, 'This people honor me with

their lips but their heart is far from me; in vain they worship me, [teaching as their doctrines the] precepts [of men' "] [Isaiah 29:13; Matthew 15:7–9; Mark 7:6–7].

IV

. . . shut up in a place . . . subordinated uncertainly . . . its weight unweighted . . . and when they were perplexed at his strange question, Jesus as he walked stood still by the edge of the Jordan [river], and extending his right hand . . . and scattered [seed] on the . . . and then . . . water . . . before [them] it brought forth fruit . . . much . . . for . . .

It is quite clear that there are reflections of the Gospel of John in the first three fragments, probably derived from the author's use of this book rather than from any oral tradition he had before him. Moreover, the presence of synoptic reminiscences in the second and third fragments points toward the author's use of all four of our canonical gospels. The story of the leper is simply expanded a bit in order to provide an explanation of how he became a leper, and the author brings in "priests" from another story which he found in Luke 17:11–19. His reliance on his memory seems to be confirmed when we notice how Jesus's indignation, found in the story of the leper in Mark, has been transferred to the author's revision—and generalization—of the story of the tribute money in the third fragment.

What we have, then, in this "unknown gospel" is simply a fictitious rewriting of gospel materials. The fourth section is too fragmentary for any sense to be derived from it. C. H. Dodd provided a reconstruction which, as Bell observed, is "not demonstrably wrong" but is not necessarily right. It is worth quoting simply as an example of what can be made of obscure fragments (I omit Dodd's brackets).[8]

[8] H. I. Bell, *Recent Discoveries of Biblical Papyri* (Oxford, 1937), 19.

When a husbandman has enclosed a small seed in a hidden place, so that it is invisibly buried, how does its abundance become immeasurable? And when they were perplexed at the strange question, then Jesus, as he walked, stood still upon the verge of the river Jordan; and stretching forth his right hand, he filled it with water and sprinkled it upon the shore; and thereupon the sprinkled water made the ground moist, and it was watered before them, and brought forth fruit.

If this is what the fragment means—and this interpretation is subject to almost limitless doubt—we should have what Bell calls "a case of miraculous germination, like the well-known mango trick of Indian jugglers." Such magic is of course not surprising in an apocryphal gospel.

All that this "gospel" reveals to us is that within the second century apocryphal revisions of the four gospels were being produced—a fact which was already known from what the Church Fathers had said about such documents. There is no reason to suppose that anything authentic about Jesus can be learned from these fragments.

Indeed, another papyrus fragment from Egypt, also published in 1935, revealed that the Gospel of John was certainly in circulation there in the early second century.[9] This tiny scrap contains John 18:31–33 and 37–38; it comes from a little book which probably contained nothing but the Fourth Gospel, though this is not certain. In any event, from this papyrus and from citations of the canonical gospels by writers both heretical and orthodox, we know that the four gospels were in circulation early in the second century and at a time earlier than the production of any of their competitors.

[9] C. H. Roberts, *An Unpublished Fragment of the Fourth Gospel in the John Rylands Library* (Manchester, 1935).

D. GNOSTIC FRAGMENTS

From 1935 until the phenomenal discoveries at Nag Hammadi, only two fragments of any importance have appeared. Both of them undoubtedly came from Gnostic groups and therefore could be disregarded by students of the life of Jesus. One was from a Coptic Gnostic document of the fourth or fifth century which contains a dialogue between the apostle John and Jesus.[10]

"Lo, I have explained unto thee, O John, concerning Adam and Paradise and the Five Trees, in an intelligible allegory."
"When I, John, heard these things, I said, 'I have made a good beginning; I have completed knowledge and a hidden mystery and allegories of truth, having been encouraged by thy love.' Now I desire further to ask thee that thou wouldest explain unto me in thy love concerning Cain and Abel: according to what fashion did Cain slay Abel? And not this only, but he was asked by him (that) spake with him, saying, Where is Abel, thy brother? But Cain denied, saying, Am I the keeper . . ."
"Lo, I have explained unto thee, O John, concerning Noah and his ark . . ."
["But I desire further to ask thee that thou wouldest] explain [unto me] concerning Me [lchizedek.] Is it not said [concerning him] that [he was] a [fatherless . . .] mother[less . . .] end of [life . . . a] priest forever. It was said [also] of him that . . .

Simply to read this fragment is enough to judge it as fictitious. Jesus is represented as the Gnostic revealer who explains the hidden meaning of the Old Testament to his favorite disciple.

In 1938 there was published a volume of Greek and Latin papyri in the John Rylands Library at Manchester, England. One papyrus fragment was obviously Gnostic-

[10] W. E. Crum, in *Journal of Theological Studies*, XLIV (1943), 176–82.

Christian in origin; it dates from the early third century, and is written in Greek.[11]

I

. . . the rest of the course of the period of the time of the Aeon they rest in silence." Having said these things, Mariamme was silent, as if the Savior had spoken up till now. Andrew says, "Brothers, what do you think about what has been spoken? For I do not believe that the Savior said these things. For they seem to have a meaning different from his thought about such matters. Was the Savior speaking secretly to a woman and not openly, so that we all might hear something worthy of consideration?"

II

. . . of the Savior." Levi says to Peter, "Peter, wrathfulness is always with you; it is present now, and so you dispute with the woman as her adversary. If the Savior considered her worthy, who are you to despise her? For he knew her fully and loved her with certainty. We should rather be ashamed and, having put on the perfect man, which was enjoined upon us, should make the Gospel proclaimed, defining nothing, and legislating nothing, as the Savior said." Having said these things, Levi went away and began to proclaim [the Gospel].

Some critics saw in this fragment a part of an unknown Gospel of the Virgin Mary; others, more judiciously, could see that the Mariamme here mentioned was probably Mary Magdalene.

In 1955 more of this gospel became known when Walter Till published three Gnostic writings from the Berlin Coptic Papyrus 8502. The path of the "unlucky star" which hovered over this papyrus from the time of its discovery has been traced in Till's edition. Carl Schmidt described the document's contents as long ago as 1896; nine years later he promised that an edition would soon appear.

[11] C. H. Roberts, *Catalogue of the Greek and Latin Papyri*, III (Manchester, 1938), 18–23 (no. 463).

Unfortunately, in 1912 a water pipe burst in the printer's cellar and ruined the plates. Schmidt began his work again, and shortly before his death in 1938 he was preparing a new edition from his old proofs. After that, Johannes Munck took over the work for a while, but during the war Hans Lietzmann entrusted it to Walter Till. Finally Till brought it to completion.

The papyrus contains three Gnostic works, all supposed to reflect revelations made by the risen Jesus. The first is the Gospel of Mariham (Mary); the second, the Apocryphon (secret book) of John, which in its original form comes from the second century; the third, the Sophia of Jesus Christ, probably based on the Apocryphon.[12]

We therefore have, in Till's edition, fifth-century Coptic versions of three Gnostic gospels or semi-gospels which go back to the second and third centuries of our era. There is no reason to suppose that any of them contains the faintest reminiscence of authentic words of Jesus. For our purposes they are worth considering only to show how alterations could be made in late Gnostic writings. If, for example, we compare the Greek version of Mariamme (Mariham) with the Coptic, we find that the words of Andrew in the first section of the Greek are assigned partly to Andrew and partly to Peter in the Coptic. Presumably a later editor broke up Andrew's speech, in order to provide somewhat more lively reading.

Again, if we look at some of the words ascribed to Jesus in the same gospel, we find that they are nothing but combinations and transformations of sayings, chiefly from the synoptic gospels. The Savior says to the disciples:

Peace be with you [John 20:19]. Receive my peace for yourselves [Matthew 10:13; Luke 10:6]. Take heed lest anyone

[12] It was Puech who noticed that among the Oxyrhynchus papyri is a Greek version (about A.D. 300) of part of the last work (P. Oxy. VIII, 1081).

lead you astray with the words, "Lo, here!" or "Lo, there!" [Matthew 24:5, 23; Luke 17:21] for the Son of Man is within you [cf., Luke 17:21]. Follow him; those who seek him will find him [cf., Matthew 7:7]. Go, therefore, and preach the Gospel of the Kingdom [Mark 16:15]. I have left no commandment but what I have commanded you [cf., John 13:34], and I have given you no law, as the lawgiver did, lest you be bound by it.

Apart from this collection of gospel sayings, there is nothing which is not Gnostic, perhaps Naassene, as the identification of "Kingdom" with "Son of Man" suggests.

IV

THE GNOSTICS AND THOMAS

Several of the papyri contain sayings of Jesus which we have called Gnostic in character, and Doresse, Puech, Quispel, and Cerfaux have called attention to Gnostic features in the Gospel of Thomas. If we take a closer look at Gnostic systems of thought, as well as at the whole movement called Gnosticism, we may be in a better position to appreciate the nature of such sayings. We may be able to discover what the environment of Thomas was.

Most of what has been known of Gnosticism comes from the writings of the Church Fathers who attacked it. Indeed, a good deal of the Christian literature from the late second century and the early third century is devoted to criticism of the tenets of various Gnostic sects. As the Fathers pointed out the errors of their opponents, they also worked out the implications of their own faith—and they described the Gnostic systems in considerable detail. The earliest writer we know who is vitally concerned with this problem is Irenaeus, bishop of Lyons in about 180. Another is Hippolytus, bishop of Rome about 230. A third is Epiphanius, bishop of Salamis in Cyprus about 375.

Irenaeus was deeply concerned with the problem because he saw the inroads that Gnosticism was making among his people in Gaul. A strong defender of the "apostolic tradition" which had been derived from his New

Testament, practically identical with ours, he believed that this tradition had been preserved by bishops and presbyters appointed by apostles and their successors. He held that it was summed up in something very much like the Apostles' Creed. And he held that Gnostics wrongly denied the unity of God and of his revelation in the Old and New Testaments; for a reasonable, balanced faith they substituted esoteric speculations. They denied the potential goodness of the world which God had made and turned to dreams of a divine spark within themselves.

Hippolytus was disturbed by the Gnostics because they were substituting philosophical speculation for Christianity. He took pains to trace the philosophical origin of each of the sects he discussed, often exaggerating the link between philosophy and Gnosticism, but drawing attention to an aspect which Irenaeus had not dealt with so fully.

Epiphanius, a militant defender of the orthodox settlement outlined at the Council of Nicaea in 325, was especially impressed by the varieties of Gnostic heresy. In his youth some women who were devotees of Gnosticism had attempted to lead him astray, and he never forgot the horror he had felt as he rejected their invitation. In his enormous *Panarion,* or "breadbasket," he described no fewer than eighty heresies, carefully comparing each one with a species of snake.

These three writers have provided most of our information about the Gnostics, and, in spite of the new discoveries, their descriptions are still invaluable. Though both Epiphanius and Hippolytus made use of Irenaeus's work, they also used authentic Gnostic sources.

What was Gnosticism? The term is modern; it is used to cover a confusing variety of sects which arose late in the first century of our era and spread from Syria and Egypt out into the rest of the Graeco-Roman world. According to the Fathers, the first Gnostic was the Simon

Magus of whom we read in the eighth chapter of Acts. There he is described by followers as "the Power which is called Great," and it may be that Luke is hinting that he regarded himself as a savior. In any event, this idea is made explicit by such second-century writers as Justin (about 150) and Irenaeus. They say that, in Simon's opinion, he had come down from heaven to redeem his followers by giving them knowledge (gnosis). Here we find the elements which are present, one way or another, in all Gnostic systems. There is a redeemer from heaven; he gives, to those who are "by nature" capable of salvation, the knowledge which *is* salvation. The Gnostic knows who he is (a spiritual being), whence he has fallen, and whither he will return.

Such knowledge has often been confused with Christianity, especially when the Christian faith in God as the creator and redeemer of all mankind has been weakened. The earliest Christianity, arising as it did out of Judaism, held firmly to the belief that God had acted in the past, was acting in the present, and would continue to act in the future. Some Christians, like some Jews, devised overprecise timetables for God's future action, and when the coming of the end of the world was delayed, they took refuge in dualistic spirituality. Losing the Christian faith in the return of Christ or the Jewish faith in the coming of God's Anointed, they looked only for the escape of the divine spark or true self from an evil world of matter and sin. At this point they became vulnerable to speculations derived from Greek philosophy or Oriental religions. They became vulnerable to Gnosticism. They became Gnostics.

To be sure, orthodox Christianity itself was modified in this direction to a considerable measure. By the early third century we find Christian teachers explicitly stating that Jesus's sayings about the future do not refer to the coming of God's kingdom on earth but to the time when individuals leave the earth by dying. In spite of such statements, however, the Church generally retained a faith which was at least close to what the apostles had believed. The Creeds speak of the future resurrection or of the life of the world to come.

Against the Church, the Gnostics often claimed that they themselves were the only ones who understood what Jesus had really meant. To be sure, in the systems of Simon Magus and his disciple Menander (early second century), the redeemer is either Simon or Menander. The other Gnostics attached themselves to the Christian tradition about Jesus as the redeemer and claimed that most of his disciples had misunderstood him. Only a Gnostic could understand the Gnostic meaning of Jesus's revelation, and this revelation had been given to a few of his disciples, after the resurrection; they had handed it down secretly to those who were worthy of receiving it.

For this reason we find among the Nag Hammadi books no fewer than three versions of the Apocryphon (secret book) of John, three Apocalypses of James, an Apocalypse of Paul, and an Apocalypse of Peter. These documents represent Christian apostles as deliverers of secret Gnostic doctrine. In addition, there are revelations ascribed to Old Testament figures such as Adam and Seth, as well as secret teachings supposed to have come from the Graeco-Egyptian god Hermes and even from Zoroaster. The Gnostics who possessed this library evidently believed that they were the heirs of a universal revelation, not just a Christian one. They believed that all the secret traditions of the mysterious East could contribute to their salvation.

In their collection, however, Christian—or semi-Christian —tradition is reflected by the presence of three gospels. One of these was published at Zurich in 1956 by Malinine, Puech, and Quispel; it is a mystical treatise entitled the Gospel of Truth, and its editors have argued that it is the book of the same title mentioned by Irenaeus and Tertullian, anti-heretical Christian writers of the second and third centuries. It was used by the Valentinians, Gnostics of the mid-second century, and may even have been written by their founder Valentinus. It is not a gospel in the ordinary sense, for it consists chiefly of meditations on the meaning of the salvation given in Jesus, and on the mystical significance of his name. Another gospel is ascribed to Philip, but, like the Gospel of Truth, it does not resemble the Church's gospels. Puech has given some quotations from it in a recent study. "We were Hebrews, we were orphans, and we no longer had a mother. But since we became Christians, we again have father and mother." The gospel discusses the fate and the salvation of the soul and seems to reinterpret themes already found in our gospels.[1] The third of the Nag Hammadi gospels is the Gospel of Thomas.

The Gospel of Thomas, too, is unlike our gospels. It consists of nothing but sayings of Jesus, more than a hundred in number, introduced by these words: "These are the secret words which Jesus the Living spoke and (which) Didymus Judas Thomas wrote. And He said, He who will find the interpretation of these words will not taste death." The idea that Jesus spoke secretly with his disciples is, of course, not specifically Gnostic. We find it expressed in the Gospel of Mark, where Jesus tells them that the secret of the kingdom of God belongs to them, while for outsiders everything takes place in parables (Mark 4:11); again, in the same gospel we read that Jesus explained the meaning of his parables to the disciples in private (Mark 4:34). It must be confessed, however, that among the Gnostics there was a much stronger emphasis on secrecy than there was among ordinary Christians, and

[1] Puech in W. Schneemelcher-E. Hennecke, *Neutestamentliche Apokryphen,* I (Tübingen, 1959), 197-99.

that the Gnostic idea of salvation through knowing something—here, the interpretation of Jesus's words—is expressed in this Preface to the gospel.

The name Didymus Judas Thomas presents some difficulties. "Didymus" in Greek and "Thomas" in Aramaic
have the same meaning: "twin." And when, in the Gospel
of John (the only canonical gospel to mention Thomas),
Thomas is described as "Thomas called Didymus" (11:16;
20:24, 29; 21:2) the evangelist is simply translating his
Aramaic name into Greek. Oriental writers and Westerners
using Oriental documents identify Judas with Thomas and
thus speak either of Judas Thomas or of Judas Didymus.[2]
Only two documents, apart from our Gospel of Thomas,
use the full name Judas Thomas Didymus or speak of Judas
Thomas as the twin—of Jesus! The first form is found in the
apocryphal Acts of Thomas, written in Syria or perhaps at
Edessa in the second or third century; the second occurs
in the Book of Thomas the Athlete, part of the Nag Hammadi collection. Puech and Doresse have rightly argued
that this form of the name suggests that the Gospel of
Thomas originated in, or near, Syria. In addition, Puech
has shown that many of the sayings in the Gospel of
Thomas are reflected in the Acts of Thomas.[3]

But something more can be said about the apostle's
name. It was Puech who first observed that the Gospel of
Thomas finally made clear what the Oxyrhynchus sayings
fragments were; for he pointed out that P. Oxy. 654
contains a Greek version of the Preface and the first six
sayings found in Thomas; P. Oxy. 1 contains Sayings 27–
28, 77 (last two lines), and 30–34; and P. Oxy. 655 gives
us a longer Greek version of Sayings 37–40. In addition,
another piece of the last papyrus contains two words which
come from Saying 25. In other words, these Oxyrhynchus

[2] Puech, CRAcInscr, 1957, 154; Doresse, 39–40.
[3] CRAcInscr, 155–56.

papyri contain parts of the Gospel of Thomas in a Greek version no later than the early third century—about the time when Origen was condemning the gospel. One might assume that the Greek version (since as a whole Thomas was probably written in Greek) was earlier than the complete Coptic version. And if this assumption is correct, it is significant that the apostle's name in the Greek fragment of the preface must be Judas Thomas; there is no space, in the fragmentary opening lines, for "Didymus." Perhaps we can begin to recover the prehistory of the Gospel of Thomas. It may be that before it reached its present state it was available in a less Gnostic, more "orthodox" form.

A comparison of all the Oxyrhynchus sayings with the Gospel of Thomas reveals that there is not much difference between them. The Coptic version mentions being "troubled" in Saying 1, but it is not certain whether this was added in Coptic or deleted in Greek. The Coptic speaks of "knowing yourselves" and "being known" in Saying 2, while the Greek says that one who knows himself will find it—the kingdom of the Father. Here the Coptic seems closer to the Pauline idea of being known by God, while the Greek simply speaks of finding the kingdom. In Saying 28, the Coptic speaks of "the kingdom," while the Greek calls it "the kingdom of God."

The differences are more marked in Saying 31.

COPTIC	GREEK
Where there are three gods, they are gods.	Where there are [two, they are not] without God,
Where there are two or one, I am with him.	and
(77) Split wood: I am there.	where there is one alone, I say, I am with him.
Lift up the stone, and you will find me there.	Lift the stone, and there you will find me;
	Split the wood, and there I am.

We cannot determine which of the two versions is the earlier, though the Coptic may simply be a mistranslation of the Greek.

The Greek version of Saying 37 is considerably longer than its Coptic equivalent.

COPTIC	GREEK
Do not take care	[Do not take care]
from morning to evening	from morning to evening
and from evening to morning	or from evening to morning
what you will put on yourselves.	nor
	for your food, what you will eat,
	or for your clothing, what you will wear.
	You are much better than the lilies,
	which neither card nor spin. . . .
	Having one garment, who do you . . . ?
	Who would add to your stature?
	He himself will give you your garment.

Here again, we cannot tell whether the Coptic version has omitted these words from the synoptic tradition (Matthew 6:25, 28, 27; Luke 12:22, 27, 25) or whether they have been added in Greek.

Perhaps the most striking divergence has been noted by Puech.[4] In Coptic the end of Saying 5 reads, "There is nothing which is covered which will remain without being uncovered." Unfortunately, the Greek is fragmentary at this point. It reads, "There is nothing buried which will

[4] "Un logion de Jésus sur bandelette funéraire," *RHR*, CXLVII (1955), 126–29.

not . . ." But Puech has restored it from a grave wrapping from Oxyrhynchus in the fifth or sixth century, which reads, "Jesus says, There is nothing buried which will not be raised." If this was the original reading of Thomas, then we have clear evidence of Gnostic removal of a reference to the resurrection. It is Gnostic because Gnostics insisted on the survival of the spirit, not the resurrection of the body.

Now if we follow Puech's clue and assume that a similar process of revision took place at the other points we have mentioned, we shall conclude that the Greek version is closer to Christian orthodoxy than the Coptic one, and that a Gnostic editor substituted "being known" for "finding the kingdom" in Saying 2, and deleted "of God" from "the kingdom of God" in Saying 28 (elsewhere in the Gospel of Thomas we never hear of the kingdom *of God*, as Cerfaux has pointed out [5]). By "kingdom" the final author of Thomas means self-knowledge or refers to the inner life. We may also assume that the mention of three gods in Saying 31 is due to a Gnostic editor who misunderstood or deliberately changed an earlier saying which is closer to the synoptic gospels. This editor also moved the saying about lifting the stone and splitting the wood so that it would come in a context (Saying 77) where Jesus declares that he is the All; in other words, stone and wood are parts of him. Whatever the saying may have meant originally, in the Coptic Thomas it has become a witness to pantheism. Similarly we should hold that the synoptic sayings not found in Saying 37 were deleted by the Gnostic editor because they seemed irrelevant to his main point. He was anxious to make plain that Jesus was hostile toward the body, not discussing "being unclothed and not being ashamed" (as in the Greek). His views were closer to the

[5] G. Garitte–L. Cerfaux, "Les paraboles du royaume dans l'Évangile de Thomas," Le Muséon, LXX (1957), 316.

Gospel of the Egyptians, where we read of "treading on the garment of shame," than to what we can make out of the Greek Thomas.

These points about Thomas mean that in the Coptic version we are not dealing with the original form of the gospel, but more probably with a version which has been Gnosticized. The Greek version is less Gnostic than the Coptic.

The sayings actually preserved in the Greek version do not sound very Gnostic, and it is tempting to suppose that in the early third century the Gospel of Thomas had not yet undergone the process of Gnosticizing. Such a supposition may be wrong, however, for in the scraps of P. Oxy. 655 we can read words which must be restored as "luminous" and "world"; these words come from Saying 25, which says, "There is light within a light-[luminous-] man and it illuminates the whole world." The conception of a "light-man" is definitely Gnostic; we find it in the Gnostic document *Pistis Sophia* (chapter 125), and the idea is expressed elsewhere in Thomas. "We came from the light" (Saying 51); there is light within the images which appear to man (Saying 83). In Gnostic thought, the men who are capable of being saved are those who have come from the light, not mankind in general.

Saying 25 deserves a little closer consideration, for it illustrates the way in which some of the sayings in Thomas were developed. We may compare it with some verses from the synoptic gospels.

SAYING 25	GOSPEL SAYINGS
He who has ears, let him hear!	Whoever has ears to hear, let him hear (Mark 4:23)
There is light within a light-man	The light which is within you (Matthew 6:23)
	You are the light of the world (Matthew 5:15)

71

and it illuminates the whole world;	Your whole body will be luminous (Matthew 6:22)
if it does not illuminate it, (it is) darkness.	If the light which is within you is darkness, how great is that darkness (Matthew 6:23)

It looks as if Gnostic exegetes had simply taken scattered sayings about light and had created their own theological synthesis from them. They referred the difficult language of the "Sermon on the Mount" to their own system, in which light and darkness were understood as opposites, not in ethical terms, but in relation to a cosmic dualism.

The first part of Saying 77 is plainly Gnostic in tone. "I am the light which is over everything. I am the All; (from me) the All has gone forth, and to me the All has returned." We must be careful not to claim too much, however. Jesus is the light in John 1:1–18; he is the light of the world in John 8:12. And in the second century, orthodox theologians like Theophilus of Antioch were not hesitant to speak of him as "all things" (in the plural). It is the total synthesis which makes this saying Gnostic; for it goes on to say, "Split wood: I am there. Lift up the stone, and you will find me there." Doresse has suggested, rather unconvincingly, that by "wood" and "stone" the author of Thomas has in mind the wood of Christ's cross and the stone at his tomb.[6] More probably his thought is like that expressed in the Gnostic Gospel of Eve. "In all things I am scattered, and from wherever you will, you gather me."[7] Thomas's combination of sayings suggests that he has cosmic pantheism in view, as we have already said.

Since Jesus is the light, his disciples are those who have

[6] Doresse, 188–89.
[7] Epiphanius, *op. cit.*, 26, 3, 1.

come from the light (51); since he is the All, they know the All (68). In contrast to them, Adam originated from a great power and great wealth, but he was not worthy of Jesus's disciples (85), presumably because he was merely carnal in origin, and merely psychic when he had the breath of life. He did not possess the illumination which Jesus gave.

Passages such as these show that the newly discovered Gospel of Thomas has a Gnostic atmosphere which made it unacceptable to the Christian Church. We should now consider more fully the meaning of this atmosphere. Is there an old, and possibly authentic, tradition on which Thomas relies and on which the Gnostics relied? In other words, is it possible that Thomas gives us trustworthy information about the sayings of Jesus?

V

THE ENVIRONMENT OF
THOMAS

The pertinent clues to the source and setting of the Gospel of Thomas are to be found in the sayings which are not in the canonical gospels but are reported by early Christian writers, both orthodox and Gnostic. We have already seen that fragments of Thomas are available in third-century papyri from Oxyrhynchus in Egypt; but this fact does not carry us far, since we do not know who the people were who made use of these papyri.

More important is the fact that Saying 1 is very close to what Clement of Alexandria tells us was found in the Gospel of the Hebrews. "He who seeks will not cease until he finds; when he finds, he will be astonished; when he is astonished, he will reign; when he reigns, he will rest." [1] We do not know what the context of this saying was in the Gospel of the Hebrews; Clement combines it with a quotation from Plato to the effect that the beginning of philosophy is to be found in an attitude of wonder. Perhaps we can infer that its starting point lay in the gospel saying, "Seek and ye shall find, knock and it will be opened unto you" (Matthew 7:7; Luke 11:9; Saying 92). The idea of

[1] *Strom.*, 2, 45, 5; 5, 96, 3.

astonishment may well be a Greek interpretation of the seeking; [2] the idea of reigning and resting may come from the Christian preaching of the kingdom of God. In any case, the saying is not specifically Gnostic; but it shows that Hebrews and Thomas are somehow related.

Another Saying (101) resembles what we find in Hebrews. According to Thomas, the disciples ask Jesus to pray and fast with them. Jesus asks them, "What sin, then, have I committed, or in what have I been overcome?" In Hebrews, Jesus's mother and brothers say to him, "John is baptizing for the remission of sins; let us go and be baptized by him." Jesus replies, "What sin have I committed, that I should go and be baptized by him?" The thought is approximately the same. In Thomas it is prayer and fasting which would imply that Jesus is not sinless; in Hebrews it is baptism. In both gospels Jesus denies that he has committed any sin, and insists that he has no need of any remedy for it. There is a difference between them, however. In Hebrews, Jesus does proceed to be baptized, so that his true mother, the Holy Spirit, can descend upon him; in Thomas, on the other hand, prayer and fasting are absolutely rejected. According to Saying 14, "If you fast, you will beget for yourselves a sin, and if you pray, you will be condemned." Admittedly, "When the bridegroom comes out of the bridechamber, then may you fast and pray" (101)—but such fasting and prayer are really unnecessary; truth is more significant than religious observance (5). Here it would appear that Thomas is closer to Gnostic thought than Hebrews is; we know that some Gnostics rejected prayer and fasting.[3] Perhaps he has simply taken over the question, "What sin have I committed?" from the Gospel of the Hebrews.

[2] Compare the *Traditions of Matthias*, quoted by Clement (2, 45, 4): "Marvel at things present."
[3] Clement, *Strom.*, 7, 41, 1.

75

Another saying apparently related to Hebrews is 11. Here Jesus tells the disciples that when he has left them they are to "go to James the Just, for whose sake the heaven and the earth came into existence." The Gospel of the Hebrews laid great emphasis on James the Just as the first Christian witness to the resurrection of Jesus (see page 35). And the notion that heaven and earth were made for someone's sake is a Jewish idea; in the Talmud we read that creation took place for Moses, or for Moses and Aaron, or for Abraham, or for David and the Messiah. This saying, then, is closely related to Jewish-Christian conceptions. It reminds us of "traditions" handed down among some Christians at the end of the second century. Clement of Alexandria tells us that "after the resurrection the Lord delivered the Gnosis to James the Just and John and Peter; they delivered it to the other apostles." [4] And the Naassenes, more Gnostic than Clement was, held that James the Lord's brother delivered traditions to a certain Mariamme, from whom they received them. [5]

Mariamme, presumably the same as the Mariham mentioned in Thomas (21, 112), was famous in the second century as a link in Gnostic tradition. We learn this fact not only from the Naassenes but also from the anti-Christian writer Celsus, who mentions both Mariamme and Salome. [6] Mariamme is the heroine of the Gnostic gospel which bears her name, and a vague memory of her connection with Naassenes or Ophites is still present in the apocryphal Acts of Philip (chapters 94–101), where the apostle goes with her to "the land of the snake-worshipers" (Naassenes and Ophites derived their names from Hebrew and Greek words for "snake"). Salome, an interlocutor of Jesus in Saying 62, also appears in the Gospel of the Egyp-

[4] Eusebius, H. E., 2, 1, 4.
[5] Hippolytus, op. cit., 5, 7, 1.
[6] Origen, Contra Celsum, 5, 62.

tians. These women, then, are encountered primarily in documents related to Gnostic groups. Their names do not, however, give definite proof that we are dealing with Gnosticism, for they also occur in the recently discovered Bodmer Papyrus which bears the title *Birth of Mary: Apocalypse of James.*[7] And this document reflects not Gnostic thought but popular Christian piety of the second century.

What we should conclude, then, about the saying which speaks of James the Just is that—since James is not mentioned elsewhere in the Gospel of Thomas—it may well be derived from the Gospel of the Hebrews or some similar source. The author of Thomas may have included it, because for him, as for the radical Gnostic Ebionites of the fourth century, James was remembered as opposed to the temple and its worship,[8] and therefore his memory could be invoked by anyone who rejected religious observances.

This is to say that, while Thomas may well make use of the Gospel of the Hebrews, he is not really Jewish or Jewish-Christian at all. We can find Jewish expressions in his work. For example, Saying 26 is purely Jewish. "Love your brother as your soul; keep him like the apple of your eye." The first half of the saying comes from Leviticus 19:17–18; the second includes the "apple of the eye," which is often mentioned in the Old Testament (for example, Deuteronomy 32:10). Again, the true disciple is described as one "of whom the world is not worthy" (Sayings 57, 80, 109). This expression occurs in the New Testament in Hebrews 11:38, but it is fairly common in Jewish literature of the rabbinic period. Finally, Saying 5 is clearly related to the book of Tobit. The disciples ask questions about fasting, prayer, and almsgiving, all of

---

[7] M. Testuz, *Papyrus Bodmer V* (Coligny, 1958).
[8] Epiphanius, *Pan.*, 30, 16, 7.

which are commended in Tobit 12:8. Jesus replies, "Do not speak falsely [cf., Tobit 4:6], and what you hate, do not do" (Tobit 4:15). The difference between Thomas and contemporary Judaism or Jewish Christianity is obvious. First, Thomas has omitted some crucial words from Tobit's "What you hate, do not do to another." The true Gnostic has no duties in relation to mankind as a whole; his basic responsibility is only to himself. Second, he rejects the fasting, prayer, and almsgiving which were cardinal duties not only in Judaism but also in early Christianity. The second-century homily known as 2 Clement insists on the absolute necessity of observing all three (16:4).

We see, then, that while there are points of contact between Thomas and Jewish Christianity as represented by the Gospel of the Hebrews, these points are significant only for details. They suggest that Thomas was acquainted with Jewish-Christian traditions, not that his environment was Jewish-Christian. Indeed, if we go beyond matters of religious observance, important as they are, to theological questions, we can see how far Thomas is from Jewish Christianity. In his gospel there is no mention of God's creation of the world, and—at least in the Coptic version—there is no trace of the resurrection of the dead. If Saying 43 is to be translated "Come into being as you pass away," it is plain that both creation and resurrection are denied. Human existence is not true being; true being is achieved only as human existence is transcended.

From Hebrews we turn to another apocryphal gospel of the second century, the Gospel of the Egyptians. With this gospel there are even clearer points of contact. In Saying 23 Jesus tells the disciples that they will go into the kingdom "when you make the two one, and make the inside like the outside, and the outside like the inside, and the upper side like the under side, and (in such a way) that you make the man (with) the woman a single one, in order that the man is not man and the woman is not woman." Something very close to this is quoted in 2 Clement 12:2, where we read that "when the Lord was asked by someone when his kingdom would come, he said, When the two will be one, and the outside like the inside, and the male with the female neither male nor female." According to Clement of Alexandria, approximately the same saying was to be found in the Gospel of the Egyptians: "When you tread on the garment of shame and when the two become one and the male with the female neither male nor female." [9] Finally, according to the late second-century Martyrdom of Peter, "The Lord says in a mystery, Unless you make the right like the left and the left like the right and the upper like the lower and the back like the front, you do not know the kingdom." [10] Evidently we are dealing with a fairly homogeneous group of sayings, whether they all come from Egyptians or not. "Neither male nor female" but "androgynous" is quoted from the Naassenes by Hippolytus, who also tells us that they used Egyptians. [11] From this evidence we should conclude that probably, though not certainly, Thomas made use of the Gospel of the Egyptians. The two gospels were used in Egypt.

This conclusion is reinforced when we look at Saying 38. Jesus says that the disciples will see him "when you undress yourselves and are not ashamed and take your clothing and lay them under your feet, like little children, and tread on them." We have already met "treading on the garment of shame" in the quotation from Egyptians given by Clement of Alexandria; and "casting off clothing" is mentioned by the Naassenes of Hippolytus. [12] We in-

[9] *Strom.*, 3, 92, 2.
[10] *Mart. Petri*, 9, 94 Lipsius—*Acta Petri cum Simone*, 38, 95.
[11] *Ref.*, 5, 7, 15; cf., 5, 7, 9 (but since Hippolytus tells us that the Naassenes also used Thomas, the quotation may be derived from him).
[12] *Ref.*, 5, 8, 44.

cline to think that this saying, like Saying 23, is probably derived from Egyptians—or from the traditions contained in it.

Sayings 61 and 62 probably belong together.[13] Jesus speaks of "two" who "will be resting on one bed" (Luke 17:34); he states that "the one will die, the other will live." Suddenly Salome addresses him. "Who are you, O man? Have you as from the One mounted my bed and eaten from my table?" Jesus replies, "I am he who came into existence from that which is equal; I was given the things of my Father" (cf., Matthew 11:27; Luke 10:22). Salome answers, "I am your disciple." These sayings remind us of the dialogue with Salome which, according to Clement of Alexandria, was to be found in Egyptians.[14] In this dialogue Jesus informs her that death is the consequence of "the works of the female" which he came to destroy. Perhaps we may suppose that Jesus can destroy these works because he originated not from a female but from the Father. It is no more than a possibility, however, that these sayings come from Egyptians.

From the resemblances which exist it is clear that Thomas shares with Egyptians an attitude of hostility toward the existence of sexual divisions. "Becoming one" is mentioned in three more sayings (3, 10, 24); "single ones" or "solitaries" are given blessings or promises in Sayings 16, 50, and 75. What is characteristic of them is characteristic of Jesus. "When you see the one who was not born of woman [cf., Matthew 11:11; Luke 7:28], cast yourselves down on your faces, and worship him; He is your Father" (cf., John 14:9).[15] Jesus hates his—earthly—father and mother (Saying 98; cf., Saying 56). When his disciples tell him, "Your brothers and your mother [in

[13] So Doresse, 103.
[14] *Strom.*, 3, 63, 2.
[15] Saying 15.

reverse order from that of the synoptic gospels] are standing outside," he declares that his brothers and his mother are those who do his Father's will (Saying 96).[16] The statement in Saying 98, "in truth she gave me life," is too fragmentary for us to assume that Jesus is speaking of his earthly mother; perhaps he is referring to the Holy Spirit, or to a substitute for the Holy Spirit—since the Spirit is only rarely mentioned in Thomas (Sayings 45, 54). When he says, "He who will know the Father and the Mother will be called 'the son of a prostitute'" (102), the Father is God, the "son of a prostitute" is Jesus (according to early anti-Christian slander), and the Mother is then probably the Holy Spirit.

Women should refrain from bearing children, as Thomas makes clear when he combines Luke 11:27-28 with Luke 23:29 (Saying 79). Their only hope lies in their potential ability to become men. This point is made abundantly clear in the last saying in the gospel (112). Simon Peter says, "Let Mariham go away from us. For women are not worthy of life." Jesus replies, "Lo, I will draw her so that I will make her a man, so that she too may become a living spirit which is like you men; for every woman who makes herself a man will enter into the kingdom of heaven." The idea that the Savior would not have spoken with a female disciple is expressed in the second- or third-century Gospel of Mary, as is the notion that women are to become men; [17] and the latter thought is also to be found in some tradition quoted by the second-century Valentinian Gnostic Theodotus.[18] Even the usually orthodox Church Father Origen insists that at the resurrection women will become men.[19]

[16] Matthew 12:47-50; Mark 3:32-35; Luke 8:20-21.
[17] Gospel of Mary, pp. 17-18 (cf., Pistis Sophia, 146); p. 9 (Walter Till).
[18] Clement of Alexandria, Excerpta ex Theodoto, 21, 3.
[19] Eph. comm. (Lommatzsch V, 272).

Puech has pointed out that such ideas lingered on among medieval heretics, and he has referred to the collection of documents published in 1890 by I. von Döllinger.[20] It is rather surprising that in that collection we read that "no one can be saved unless the Father draws him,"[21] that one is to be saved by "putting off the tunic,"[22] and that women are to be saved by becoming men.[23] We might almost suppose that Thomas continued to be read among these heretics, the Cathari.

Many of the ideas of Thomas, then, can be paralleled in the Gospel of the Egyptians and, to some extent, in the Gospel of Mary. It remains uncertain, however, whether Thomas is actually based on these documents or relies, like them, on traditions about Jesus which had already passed through a Gnostic environment. The parallels show, at the very least, that Thomas shares a semi-Gnostic world view which is reflected in the other books.

We have already quoted one parallel from the Valentinian Gnostics; there is another, which is very close to Saying 39. "Many times you have desired to hear these words which I speak to you, and you have no one else from whom to hear them. The days will come when you will seek me and will not find me" (John 7:34, 36). The first part of the saying is quoted from the Marcosian Valentinians by Irenaeus, late in the second century, with a few insignificant differences.[24] It looks like a development from Luke 17:22: "The days will come when you desire to see one of the days of the Son of Man, and you will not see it."[25] What has happened is that the emphasis in Jesus's

---

[20] CRAcInscr, 1957, 162, 166; v. Döllinger, *Beiträge zur Sektengeschichte des Mittelalters*, II (Munich, 1890).
[21] *Op. cit.*, 208.
[22] *Ibid.*, 210.
[23] *Ibid.*, 151–52, 176–77, 191, 219 (Puech).
[24] *Adv. haer.*, 1, 20, 2 (I, 179, Harvey).
[25] Cf. also Matthew 13:17; Luke 10:24 (A. Resch in *TU* 5, 4, 397).

words has been changed from a contrast between present and future to one between Jesus's revelation and the ignorance which exists apart from it. In other words, what was eschatological has become Gnostic.

But Valentinians were not the only Gnostics to use sayings like those in Thomas. The followers of the Egyptian Gnostic Basilides knew the saying (24) about "one from a thousand and two from ten thousand." [26] The Basilidians were evidently reflecting, as the author of Thomas does, on the infinitesimal numbers of the elect. Perhaps we can gain further insight into their teaching if we compare with this saying the similar words of Ecclesiastes (7:28): "One man among a thousand have I found"—and no women! For we know that the Basilidians also said, "We (alone) are men, but all the others are swine and dogs; and for this reason he (Jesus) said, Do not cast pearls before the swine or give what is holy to the dogs" (Matthew 7:6).[27] It looks as if the Basilidians were giving their own interpretation to the anti-feminist words of Ecclesiastes, and to a mysterious saying of Jesus. Now if this is so, it is quite likely that they were the original authors of Thomas's Saying 24; he has derived it from them. Such a conclusion would not, of course, mean that Thomas was writing at a late date. We know that Basilides flourished in the reign of Hadrian (117–138). Thomas is not necessarily much later. The significant fact, however, is that he has this saying in common with Basilides' followers.

Another Gnostic group which shares a saying with Thomas is that of the Ophites, from whom Celsus, writing against Christians about 180, gives a quotation. A very slight alteration in the Coptic text of Saying 74 is enough to bring it into exact correspondence with the Ophites'

[26] Irenaeus, *Adv. haer.*, 1, 24, 6 (I, 202); cf., *Pistis Sophia*, 134.
[27] Epiphanius, *op. cit.*, 24, 5, 2.

words, set forth in their *Heavenly Dialogue.* "How many are about the well, and none at the well." [28]

From Hippolytus we learn that the Naassenes, apparently a branch of the Ophites, definitely made use of the Gospel of Thomas; and Hippolytus gives us a quotation from it.[29] Unfortunately it is not identical with what we have in our texts of the gospel, either in Greek or in Coptic.

HIPPOLYTUS	GREEK (fragmentary)	COPTIC (Saying 3)
He who seeks me will find me in children from seven years; for there, in the fourteenth age, having been hidden I shall be manifest.	An [old] man [in his days] will not hesitate to ask [an infant of seven days] about the place of [life,][and he] will [live.]	The old man in his days will not hesitate to ask an infant of seven days about the place of life, and he will live.

As Puech says, "the resemblances are so remote and the differences so pronounced that they would almost lead one to deny any relation between the Gospel of Thomas used by the Naassenes and the one we have." [30] He suggests, however, either that the Naassenes had altered their text of Thomas or that the source used by Hippolytus was citing the gospel very freely.

There is another passage, also quoted from the Naassenes by Hippolytus,[31] which is practically identical with our Saying 10.

HIPPOLYTUS	SAYING 10
If you ate dead things and made them living, if you eat living things, what will you do?	On the days when you were eating that which is dead, you were making it as that which lives. When you come into the light, what will you do?

[28] Origen, *Contra Celsum* 8, 15–16.
[29] *Ref.*, 5, 7, 20.
[30] CRAcInscr 1957, 151; W. Schneemelcher-E. Hennecke, *op. cit.*, I, 204.
[31] *Ref.*, 5, 8, 32.

The Naassenes of Hippolytus were speaking very enigmatically ("living things" meant, in their view, "spiritual men" or "pearls" from the supreme God), and in Thomas we find simply a variant version. Our gospel substitutes "coming into the light" for "eating living things."

In speaking of the gospels of the Hebrews and of the Egyptians we have already said something of the use the Naassenes made of traditions like those in Hebrews and of Egyptians itself. Now we should endeavor to describe this Gnostic group in a little more detail. With the Ophites they shared a reverence for the snake in the garden of Eden; for this snake (sometimes identified with Christ), they believed, had been trying to persuade Adam and Eve to eat the fruit of the tree of knowledge. The Creator-God of the Old Testament—whom they regarded as hostile to true Gnostics—had thwarted the serpent's purpose, but when Christ came, he revealed the secrets of knowledge to his disciples, or at least to some of them. Because of this secret revelation, they believed that they could find traces of their gnosis not only in the Bible but also in Greek and Oriental religious documents. They read Homer and other poets in this light.[32]

According to them, the primal being is both male and female, and is to be called Man or Son of Man or Adamas. Hippolytus gives us a fragment of a hymn they used. "From thee, Father, and because of thee, Mother, the two immortal names parents of the Aeons, citizens of heaven, great-named Man." Perhaps we have a reflection of this kind of doctrine in the Gospel of Thomas (Saying 102), where we hear of "knowing the Father and the Mother."

The primal being is threefold in nature, since it consists of elements which are intelligible (spiritual), psychic (related to soul), and material. All three elements of the

[32] What we know of them is reported by Hippolytus, *op. cit.*, 5.

85

divine nature descended into one human being, Jesus who was born of Mary. They came down as three "men." and used him simply as an instrument of revelation. He did not do anything; they spoke through him, to human beings who were by nature related to each of the elements. Just as there are three kinds of human beings—angelic, psychic, and material—so now there are really three kinds of churches. There is the "elect church," consisting of Gnostics; there is the "called church" (for "many are called but few are elect"—Matthew 22:14); and there is the "captive church"—presumably related to Jesus's preaching to captives (Luke 4:18) and to Paul's notion that the Jerusalem below is enslaved (Galatians 4:24–25). The three churches, then, probably consist of Naassenes, Christians, and the rest of mankind.

Jesus proclaimed salvation, by means of knowledge, to those who were capable of receiving it. His teaching is preserved partly in secret traditions given by his brother James to a certain Mariamme, partly in the Gospel of the Egyptians, and partly in the Gospel of Thomas. Though the Naassenes may not have said so, they must have believed that this teaching was also preserved (though misunderstood) in the four gospels of the Church as well. These gospels probably contained the "psychic teaching" of Jesus. It could be correctly interpreted only by those who knew the secret traditions and the apocryphal gospels.

What Jesus taught the Naassenes was that at the beginning there was a man who was born from earth. He lay inert, without breath and without motion, like a statue. He was an image of the Man Adamas, above, but he was merely material. Finally breath was given him, as in Genesis 2:7. When he had breath he became psychic, for the substance (so to speak) of the soul is breath. He had advanced beyond the purely material, but he had not advanced very far. He tried to increase and multiply, since he did not know what the Naassenes knew—i.e., that sexual intercourse is absolutely evil. It represents man's fatal effort to become one without recognizing that the only real unity is spiritual. It is the equivalent of casting pearls before swine, of giving what is holy to dogs (cf., Saying 92). Man's true goal is to reach a state like that of the first creation, where he was made both male and female (a literal reading of Genesis 1:26–27). There is to be neither male nor female, but a new creation; man must cast off his garments (his physical body) and become one being. Since the primal being is called Man or Son of Man or Adamas, however, it can be said that all human beings must become men. When they become men and cast off their garments they recognize that the kingdom is within (Luke 17:21; cf., Sayings 2 and 111).

The Savior knew the nature of each of his disciples (John 2:25; 13:26). He therefore knew that each had to come to his own nature. And because there are twelve gates of the heavenly world, he chose twelve disciples and spoke to every tribe through them (presumably there were four disciples for each kind of human being).[33] Because human nature is so diverse, not all could hear or accept what the disciples proclaimed. "No one can come to me unless my heavenly Father draws him" (cf., Saying 112).

The emphasis which Jews and Christians lay on the resurrection of the physical body is thus a complete mistake. When Jesus said to the Pharisees, "You are whitened tombs, full of dead bones inside" (cf., Matthew 23:27; Luke 11:44), he meant that this was so because "there is not a living man within you." And when the gospels say that "the dead will come out of the tombs," they are really

[33] Four male disciples are mentioned in Thomas: Thomas himself (Preface, Sayings 12–13), James (11), Simon Peter (12, 112), and Matthew (12).

speaking of spiritual rebirth. For the Naassenes know that the gospel is spiritual; it has nothing to do with the physical and the material.

What we find in this Gnostic system is a complete spiritualization of the Christian gospel. The spiritualization is accompanied by a love of the esoteric and a love of finding the esoteric where it might not seem to be present. For our purposes it is important that the Naassenes used the Gospel of Thomas, and that so many features of their doctrine resemble what Thomas teaches.

Indeed, we may even suggest that Naassene doctrine is reflected in a mysterious saying (12–13) in which Thomas even refuses to relate what Jesus told him. Jesus had uttered three words to him; the disciples had asked what the three words were. "If I tell you one of the words he said to me," Thomas replies, "you will bring stones and you will cast them at me, and a fire will go forth from the stones and destroy you." If we start with the stones, we should point out that the Naassenes believed that stones were animate beings.[34] As for the three words, the Naassenes held that the existence of the universe depended on the utterance of the three strange, or even meaningless, Hebrew words found in Isaiah 28:10: "*Caulacau, Saulasau, Zeesar.*"[35] And we know that the Basilidian Gnostics taught that the Savior "descended in the name Caulacau."[36] Since what Thomas was discussing with Jesus was the question of what Jesus was like, these three words might seem appropriate.

When we come to discuss the use which various Gnostic groups made of the sayings of Jesus found in our canonical gospels we shall meet the Naassenes again. Here it is enough to say that in many respects they seem to be re-

---

[34] Hippolytus, *op. cit.*, 5, 7, 10.
[35] *Ibid.*, 5, 8, 5.
[36] Irenaeus, *Adv. haer.*, 1, 24, 6 (I, 202, Harvey).

markably close to the doctrines which are set forth in the Gospel of Thomas.

Further similarities exist between Thomas and Gnostic documents, but perhaps we need not trace them all in any detail, especially since Puech has proved that Thomas was known to the Manichees,[37] and most of the other Gnostic writings we might mention are post-Manichaean. Enough evidence has been given to show that *as a whole* Thomas must be considered a Gnostic gospel.

Thus far we have laid emphasis only on what Thomas has in common with apocryphal and Gnostic writings. There is another side to the story, however: we must also consider the non-canonical sayings which occur not in Gnostic but in orthodox writers. We have already seen that in 2 Clement there is no hesitation about using materials which are later (?) found in Egyptians and in Thomas as well. Another example is provided by the apologist Justin, who wrote about 160. "The new law wished us to 'sabbatize' [keep the Sabbath] constantly." [38] By "the new law" Justin seems to mean the teaching of Jesus; and such a commandment is to be found in Thomas, Saying 28. Again, Irenaeus quotes as a saying of Jesus, "Blessed is he who existed before he was made man"—and approximately the same words are found in Saying 19.[39] Clement of Alexandria apparently alludes to Saying 28; [40] and we have already seen that the semi-orthodox Martyrdom of Peter, contemporary with him, has several close parallels with Thomas.[41] In a third-century "Manual of Christian discipline," the *Didascalia Apostolorum* (page 134, Connolly), Saying 49 is exactly reproduced.

[37] CRAcInscr 1957, 165–66.
[38] Justin, *Dial.*, 12, 3.
[39] Irenaeus, *Epideixis*, 43 (tr. J. P. Smith, cf., 182 *n.* 207); the saying is ascribed to Jeremiah by Lactantius, *Div. inst.*, 4, 8.
[40] *Strom.*, 3, 99, 4.
[41] *Mart. Petri*, 9 (Saying 23); 10 (Sayings 17 and 77).

Perhaps the most interesting reflections of these sayings, however, are provided by Origen (third century) and Augustine (fourth and fifth centuries). Origen says, "I have read somewhere that the Savior said—and I wonder whether someone has fictitiously assumed the role of the Savior, or has recalled these words from memory, or if it is true that this was said—that the Savior himself said, He who is near me is near the fire; he who is far from me is far from the kingdom." [42] Origen's hesitation can readily be explained. In a homily on Luke he vigorously condemned the Gospel of Thomas as apocryphal; [43] he could hardly say in another homily that he was relying on what he had read in it. Augustine rejects another saying absolutely. "When the apostles were asking what they should think about the prophets of the Jews who were thought to have predicted, in the past, something about his coming, our Lord, disturbed because they still had such ideas, replied, You have left the Living One who is before you and you have spoken concerning the dead. What is remarkable," Augustine continues, "when my opponent has brought this testimony forth from some apocryphal writings or other, if the heretics have invented such things about the prophets, since they do not accept the prophetic writings?" [44] The "testimony" is evidently Saying 53 in Thomas, but Augustine has no hesitation about declaring it to be fictitious.

In the latter half of the second century the Christian Church had already rejected, in principle, such apocryphal gospels as that of Thomas by insisting that only the four-fold gospel "canon" was authoritative; only the four gospels ascribed to Matthew, Mark, Luke, and John could

---

[42] *Jer. hom.*, 20, 3; Migne, PG 13, 531D–32A. The saying (*n.* 82) is quoted from Origen by Didymus of Alexandria (PG 39, 1488D).
[43] *Luc. hom.*, 1, p. 5 Rauer.
[44] Augustine, *C. Advers. leg. et proph.*, 2, 14; Migne, PL 42, 647.

be read in the worship of the Christian communities. To be sure, Clement of Alexandria occasionally made use of apocryphal writings, but in the next generation Origen was much more careful to differentiate the true from the false. He tells us, in the homily on Luke we have already mentioned, that the Church's "approved moneychangers" [45] selected only four gospels out of the many which were available—and one of those which they rejected was that entitled "according to Thomas." Early in the fourth century, Eusebius of Caesarea also stated that the Gospel of Thomas was to be rejected because it was ascribed to an apostle by heretics; [46] and Cyril of Jerusalem informed catechumens that the Manichees had written this gospel. [47] It is true that the Manichees were very fond of Thomas; it is not true, however, that they wrote it—the testimony of Origen is enough to prove that it is pre-Manichaean.

The Church was thus able to reject the Gospel of Thomas as a whole. Origen's embarrassment in relation to Saying 82, however, shows that the problem of judging various items contained within such gospels had not been solved. It was perfectly possible for a late document to contain early materials, and for a forgery to reflect authentic traditions. The fact that as a whole Thomas reflects a Gnostic environment does not permit us to say that everything it contains is to be rejected. In the late second century Irenaeus tried to solve the problem by analyzing the method—literary and theological—of the Gnostic gospel writers. According to him, they "read from unwritten sayings [agrapha] and, as the saying goes, undertake to weave ropes from sand; they transfer materials and reshape them and, by making one thing out of another, they lead many

[45] Oddly enough, the expression "approved moneychangers" is derived from a non-canonical saying ascribed to Jesus.

[46] H. E., 3, 25, 6.

[47] Catech., 4, 36; Migne, PG 33, 500B.

astray by the evilly devised fantasy of their compilations of the Lord's words." He went on to compare their work with that of someone who finds a mosaic portrait of a king. This forger destroys the authentic portrait and uses the bits of mosaic to make a picture of a dog or a fox—and then claims that he has reconstructed the king's portrait! [48]

Irenaeus's analysis is highly satisfactory, provided one agrees that he knows what the king really looks like. For this knowledge, Irenaeus relied on what he called the apostolic tradition, handed down in the books of prophets and apostles, transmitted by teachers who were successors of the apostles, and summarized in the Church's credal formulas. The tradition was publicly known, not taught in secret by a few; it was authoritative, for it had been delivered by Christ to his apostles and by them to their successors. To this claim the Gnostics naturally replied that their tradition was authoritative, and indeed more authoritative than the tradition generally accepted; it was secret because Jesus had intended it to be secret.

Historical analysis can give some assistance in settling this kind of debate, but the ultimate issue is both historical and theological. The question is whether one accepts the king's portrait as painted by the Church or the various portraits painted by the Gnostic teachers of the second century. If it should appear that the Gnostic portraits are ultimately based on the Church's gospels, along with some distortions added by the Gnostics themselves, then the greater antiquity of the Church's picture of Jesus should lead to its acceptance on historical grounds. Even if some of the Gnostic materials should seem to be thoroughly trustworthy, they can be accepted by the Church only with the greatest caution. Those who transmitted such materials did not stand within the Christian community;

[48] *Adv. haer.*, 1, 8, 1 (I, 66–67, Harvey).

they did not value what the Church valued; they created what the apostle Paul calls "another gospel" (Galatians 1:6). They proclaimed "another Jesus" (2 Corinthians 11:4).

For this reason, our consideration of the environment of Thomas is an important first step toward the analysis of the gospel and its materials. It suggests that we must proceed with extreme care to look at the "secret words of Jesus" contained in it, for there is always the possibility that, as Origen says, someone may have fictitiously assumed the role of the Savior, or that the sayings may have been garbled in transmission.

VI

THE GNOSTICS AND
OUR GOSPELS

If the Gospel of Thomas reflects the atmosphere of the
Gnostic sects of the second and third centuries, we may
well ask what use these Gnostic sects made of the gospels
recognized by the Church. Is there any correlation between the ways in which Gnostics used them and the ways
in which gospel-type sayings are transmitted in Thomas?
It is fairly certain that the methods employed are approximately the same. Sometimes the Gnostics combined
materials derived from various gospels simply for the sake
of completeness; sometimes they combined them and rearranged them, in order to make their special theological
points. Since they believed that they possessed the true
understanding of Jesus's teaching, they felt free to restate
what he had taught so that its Gnostic significance would
become clear.

In the middle of the second century a sect known as
the Carpocratians held that "Jesus spoke in a mystery [or
"secret"] privately to his disciples." What he spoke about
was presumably the Carpocratian system; but the Carpocratians were probably justifying their idea by appealing
to the Church's gospels. The mention of "mystery" is

found in Mark 4:11; and "privately" occurs in Mark 4:34. Irenaeus gives us one extensive example of their exegesis, and of the text they used. First the text.

When you are with your adversary on the way,	Matthew 5:25
take pains to be freed from him,	Luke 12:58
lest he give you to the judge,	Matthew 5:25
and the judge to the servant,	
and he cast you in prison.	Luke 12:58
Verily, I say to you, you will not come out	Matthew 5:26
from there until you pay the last quadrant.	

This oscillation between the two gospels may be based on either a primitive harmony of the gospels or on a manuscript of either one in which readings from the other were to be found. The Carpocratians' exegesis, however, seems to show that they were consciously choosing from each gospel the items which they found useful. The "adversary" is the devil, one of the angels in this world, who leads souls astray to the "prince," the first of the creator-angels. The "prince" is not mentioned in the verses Irenaeus has quoted, but he is to be found in Luke, not in Matthew. Moreover, the idea of being freed from the adversary (Luke) is very different from that of being reconciled to him (Matthew). The "servant" (Matthew; Luke has the official term *practor*) is the servant of the creator-angel, and his service is that of transferring souls from one body to another—the "prison" is the body. "Come out from there" means to escape from the body to the God who is above the creator-angels. "Pay the last quadrant" means to undergo all the humiliation of which the body is capable. (We do not know why the Carpocratians preferred Matthew's "quadrant" to Luke's "lepton"; both are very small coins, but perhaps the quadrant was better-known in the Roman world.) [1]

[1] Irenaeus, *Adv. haer.*, 1, 25, 4–5 (I, 208–9, Harvey).

95

This exegesis seems to show (1) that the text the Carpocratians used is not fully reproduced by Irenaeus; but also (2) that it was based on careful selection of items from each of the two gospels they were explaining at this point.

Similarly, we know that Marcion, who taught at Rome about the same time, used only the Gospel of Luke and tried to free it from interpolations. In his opinion it was more Jewish than the authentic gospel of Jesus, for the apostles—with the exception of Paul—tried to present the gospel in such a way as to appeal to Jews. They thus corrupted it. Unfortunately, Marcion's critical work seems to have been entirely subjective. There is no evidence that he used any other gospel or traditional source for sayings of Jesus, even though some of his omissions could have arisen as a result of comparing Luke with John.

The contemporary Valentinians had their own Gospel of Truth, mentioned by Irenaeus,[2] and found among the Nag Hammadi documents; as Irenaeus says, its form is quite different from that of the Church's gospels. In addition, they used the four canonical gospels, not altering the text but changing the meaning, especially in regard to the parables, by explaining that everything Jesus said really referred to Valentinian doctrine. Impressed by the frequency with which groups of three occur in the parables, they usually said that such groups reflected their own view that there were three classes of men: those with spirit, those with soul, and those who were merely material.[3] One disciple of Valentinus, named Ptolemaeus, produced the earliest bit of exegesis we possess for the opening verses of the Gospel of John; another, Heracleon, wrote notes on at least the first eight chapters of the same book. These facts indicate that the Valentinians generally

[2] *Adv. haer.*, 3, 11, 9 (II, 52, Harvey).
[3] C. Barth, *Die Interpretation des Neuen Testaments in der valentinianische Gnosis* (Leipzig, 1911), 30–31; 60–67.

relied on exegesis of the Church's books, rather than on revision of them, in order to make them their own.[4] To be sure, the Valentinians claimed that they possessed secret traditions; but they do not seem to have produced new gospels like the canonical ones. In this regard they were like the Essenes, who provided their own exegesis of the Old Testament. The Gospel of Truth does not represent itself as having been written by an apostle. We should conclude that the Valentinians regarded apocryphal gospels with much the same caution as that exhibited by more orthodox Christians. One Valentinian teacher, named Marcus, told an apocryphal story about Jesus's infancy; [5] but such quotations are rare among them.

On the other hand, when we come to the Naassenes (late second century or early third), we find significant examples of Gnostic interweaving.[6]

Unless you drink my blood and eat my flesh	Unless you eat the flesh and drink the blood of the Son of Man (John 6:53); my flesh . . . my blood (6:54–56)
you will not enter into the kingdom of heaven;	you will not enter into the kingdom of heaven (Matthew 5:20; 18:3).
but if you drink the cup which I drink,	Can you drink the cup which I drink? (Mark 10:38)
where I go, there you cannot enter.	Where I go, you cannot come (John 8:21; 13:33).

Here the process of interweaving is obvious; the purpose of the process is not so obvious. According to Hippolytus, the Naassenes taught that "living things" were "reasons, intelligences, men—pearls which the great undif-

---

[4] Tertullian (De praescr. haer., 28) makes the same observation.
[5] Irenaeus, Adv. haer., 1, 20, 1 (I, 177–78).
[6] Hippolytus, 5, 8, 11.

ferentiated Being has cast into the work here below."
They held that men were to eat such living things (see
Saying 10), but since they understood this "eating" as a
spiritual process, they undoubtedly held that drinking
the blood of Jesus and eating his flesh was spiritual too
(cf., John 6:63: "The Spirit is what gives life, the flesh
is of no avail; the words which I have spoken to you are
spirit and life"). But why were Jesus's disciples not to
drink the cup which he drank? Perhaps the Naassenes
were so much concerned with "spiritual" meanings that
they wished to reject the possibility of taking part in a
real Eucharist, with real wine and real bread. To drink
the cup which Jesus drank would mean surrender to the
carnal practices of the "psychic" Church. In any event, it
is clear that they themselves created this compilation
from the Church's gospels.

The Naassenes' version of the parable of the sower (Matthew 13:18–23; Mark 4:3–9; Luke 8:5–8) [7] is based on a
combination of Matthew and Luke, though without any
really significant alterations. They explained it as meaning
that "these mysteries are understood only by the perfect
Gnostics"—an interpretation based on Matthew 13:19,
which speaks of those who "hear the message of the kingdom and do not understand it." At one point, however,
their exegetical ingenuity was responsible for the combination they made. Matthew speaks of the "fair" soil on
which some seed was cast; Luke uses the word "good."
The Naassenes found both adjectives in Deuteronomy
31:20, where Moses speaks of the "fair and good land" to
which he will lead his people. Since they used the Deuteronomy passage to explain the parable, they used both
adjectives in speaking of the sower's soil. Once more, their
combinations are due to their theological intentions.

Another quotation apparently reflects a different pur-

[7] *Ibid.*, 5, 8, 29–30.

pose. The Naassenes quoted the question of Jesus, "Why do you call me good?" from either Mark 10:18 or Luke 18:19 (Matthew 19:17 has a different question). They gave his answer, "One is good," from Matthew 19:17, however, since the expressions used in Mark and Luke are different. All three synoptic gospels continue with an admonition to obey the commandments of God. The Naassenes, on the other hand, turned to Matthew 5:45, which urges men to become sons of "your Father who is in heaven," who "makes his sun rise on the evil and the good and makes it rain on the just and the unjust." They changed "your Father" to "my Father" and altered the saying so that the sun would rise on the just and the unjust and the rain would fall on the pious and on sinners. What they were doing was, apparently, simply changing the gospel sequence in order to suggest that their version was more reliable than that of the gospels. They also removed a command to obey the injunctions of the Decalogue.

Another kind of modification is brought out in their rearrangement of Matthew 7:13–14. The gospel mentions a narrow gate; then it speaks of the broad road to destruction; finally it refers to the narrow entrance to life. Partly in order to smooth out the sequence of thought, but also partly to emphasize the narrowness of the way to life, the Naassenes reversed the order of the last two parts of the saying. Similarly, when they quoted John 4:21–24 they rearranged the order of the verses. "God is a Spirit [24]; therefore the true worshipers [23] will worship neither on this mountain nor in Jerusalem [21] but in spirit [23]." The sense of the passage in John is not significantly changed, but the new order leads more precisely to the Naassene conclusion: "For the worship of the Perfect is spiritual, not fleshly."

A good example of their work of synthesis is provided in their combination of two gospel sayings. "A light is not

99

laid under a bushel but on a lamp stand; we proclaim the proclamation on the rooftops, on all roads and all streets, and even in houses." The saying about the bushel and the lamp stand is found in Matthew 5:15 and Luke 11:33; the word "light" occurs in the preceding verse in Matthew. But "light" is also mentioned in Matthew 10:27 and Luke 12:3; and in both gospels Jesus goes on to say, "What you hear in your ear proclaim [or "will be proclaimed"] on the roofs." The sayings have been combined as the result of a kind of verbal association, though theological interpretation is also a factor.

This example is important because the same combination, though in reverse order, is to be found in Saying 34 in Thomas. "What you hear in your ear preach to another ear upon your roofs. For no one lights a lamp and puts it under a bushel . . . but he puts it on the lamp stand."

We know that the Naassenes were fond of such combinations, because Hippolytus describes one rather elaborate one. It began with the story of Jesus's transforming water into wine and thus manifesting "the kingdom of heaven" (John 2:1–11—though John says he manifested "his glory"). The Naassenes claimed that this passage showed that the kingdom is "within you" (Luke 17:21), and they added that the same doctrine was expressed in the parables which compared the kingdom with a treasure (Matthew 13:44) and with leaven in three measures of meal (Matthew 13:33). It is worth noting that, though Thomas contains no miracle stories, in it we find the kingdom within (Saying 2), the parable of the treasure (106), and the parable of the leaven (93).

In Naassene transmission and exegesis of the sayings of Jesus there is a tendency to combine words found in different contexts in order to bring out their Gnostic meaning. We also find a tendency to rearrange the sequences found in the gospels, even within individual sayings. To some extent, this rearrangement may be due simply to the shortcomings of memory. It is also probably to be ascribed to the Naassenes' desire to show that they possess the true understanding of the sayings, an understanding different from that possessed by ordinary Christians.

We have also seen that the Naassenes, who knew and used the Gospel of Thomas, quote several gospel sayings in a way which seems to reflect Thomas. It must be admitted, however, that their version of the parable of the sower is different from that which Thomas provides (Saying 8). Perhaps the difference is due to the development which took place between the early third century, when Hippolytus described the Naassenes, and the fourth century, when our manuscript of Thomas was written. On the other hand, the Naassenes may well have used different sources at different times or on different occasions.

The importance of their work for our study lies in the similarity of the methods they used with what seems to be the method of Thomas.

VII

THOMAS AS AUTHOR
AND THEOLOGIAN

A. THE METHOD OF THOMAS

In form, the sayings contained in the Gospel of Thomas fulfill the expectation which a reader would derive from the Preface to the book. Since they are words spoken by "Jesus the Living," the reader would expect to find that they resembled what is to be found in the Church's gospels. Since they are secret words, he would expect most of them to be at least slightly different from what was known publicly. And, since a blessing is given to him "who will find the interpretation of these words," the reader would expect to find many of them mysterious, or at least set in a new context which makes understanding difficult. All these features are to be found in the sayings and in their arrangement.

In Thomas there are "sayings" of Jesus, including blessings and woes, questions, suppositions ("if" or "when" or "where"), commands, predictions, and general statements. This situation is just what we find in the Church's gospels, and it does not help us to establish any criteria of authenticity.

There are also parables, just as in the gospels of Mat-

thew, Mark, and Luke—and indeed, almost all of the
twenty-four parables in Thomas are very closely related to
those in the other books.

Finally, there are dialogues, mostly between Jesus and
the group of his disciples, although—just as in the Church's
books—sometimes individuals are named, such as Simon
Peter (Sayings 12, 112), Matthew (12), Thomas (12–13),
Mariham (21), and Salome (62). Occasionally the inter-
locutors are simply "they" (91, 97, 101), and once an
unidentified woman is mentioned (79), just as in the parallel in Luke (11:27).

In other words, the form of these sayings is intended
to give an impression of authenticity. Extensive revelations
of cosmic secrets might be characteristic of a "just angel,"
but in Saying 12 Simon Peter is not commended for comparing Jesus with such a being. More logical discourses
might be expected from a philospher, but only Matthew
calls Jesus a wise philosopher in this book. Jesus speaks
in a manner which reminds, and probably is intended to
remind, the reader of the way he speaks in the canonical
gospels.   .

In the synoptic gospels we find two similar expressions,
"He who has ears to hear, let him hear," and, "He who has
ears, let him hear," associated with Jesus's teaching in
parables. The expressions are intended to call the hearer's
attention both to what Jesus is saying and to what he
means by it. In just the same way, Thomas makes use of
both of them when he relates parables which are close
to those in the synoptic gospels (Sayings 7, 22, 64, 66, 93),
and also when he sets forth a Gnostic saying (25) which is
based on synoptic materials.

To analyze the Gospel of Thomas on the basis of the
literary forms it employs, however, does not do us much
good. This is so for several reasons. (1) Parallels to the
canonical gospels are present, in much the same propor-

tions, in sayings, parables, and dialogues alike. (2) The theological themes discussed in all three forms are much the same. (3) "Formal" analysis of the synoptic gospels provides practically no criteria for judging authenticity, and it is not likely to carry us very far in dealing with Thomas. It should be added that sayings, parables, and dialogues are to be found in most of the apocryphal gospels which we know.

Perhaps we can get a little farther if we look at the way in which some of the materials in Thomas are arranged. Garitte has pointed out that nearly half the sayings are related to others in sequence, usually in pairs, by verbal association.[1] This phenomenon, observable in the synoptic gospels as well (a conspicuous example is found in Mark 9:34–50), seems to point toward oral transmission of the sayings. Rabbinic and Christian teachers often helped their students to remember things, and sometimes the students helped themselves, by arranging materials so that one key word would lead to another. In Thomas there is a conspicuous example of this process in Sayings 59–62. The key words seem to be "life" (59), leading to "the Living One" and "live" (60); this saying also mentions "die," and it goes on to speak of a limb and of a man who dies; the man has no place within for "rest." Saying 61 mentions dying, living, and resting on a bed; then comes Saying 62, where Salome speaks to Jesus about a bed. This sequence may well have been handed down by word of mouth.

The connections between other groups of sayings are more complicated. For instance, Saying 21 is a parable which is not found in the canonical gospels. It tells of children living in a field. The "masters of the field" come and say, "Leave our field to us." After this parable comes another (Saying 22), clearly parallel to Matthew 24:42–

[1] Garitte, in Le Muséon, LXX (1957), 63–64.

43. But if we look at what precedes this parable in Matthew, we discover that in Matthew 24:40 "two in a field" are mentioned, and in Matthew 24:42 the Master comes. It seems reasonable to conclude that Thomas has based his new parable of the children in the field on items already collected by Matthew. The sequence of Sayings 21 and 22, in this case, is based on the sequence in Matthew.

Again, Garitte observes that Sayings 26 and 27 are tied together by the mention of "eye" in both of them. But we can add that in the synoptic parallels to Saying 25 the eye is also mentioned, though not in Thomas's Gnosticizing version. This point seems to show at least that Thomas was relying, at this point, on an earlier compilation of sayings in which there were three sayings about the eye, not two.

Saying 66 is a slightly modified version of the parable of the vineyard, which is related in all three synotic gospels (Matthew 21:33–46; Mark 12:1–12; Luke 20:9–19). Thomas concludes it, as none of them does, with the words, "He who has ears, let him hear!" Then, as a separate Saying (67), he has Jesus say, "Instruct me concerning this stone which the builders rejected; it is turning into a cornerstone." But this is what the three synoptic evangelists provide as the conclusion of the parable of the vineyard. Thomas's separation of it from the parable seems thoroughly artificial.

The fourteenth saying is another one which reflects a process of compilation. It begins with the rejection of fasting, prayer, and almsgiving; then it turns to the question of dietary observances. "And if you go into every land, and travel in the regions, if they receive you, eat what they set before you." Thus far the instructions are closely parallel to those given Christian missionaries in Luke 10:1, 8. An explanation for eating anything set before one comes next; it is almost identical with that stated in

Matthew 15:11. But before giving this explanation, Thomas inserted the words, "Heal the sick among them." This command has nothing whatever to do with the subject he is discussing, and it breaks the continuity of his thought into pieces. Why did he include it? Because it is found in Luke 10:9, directly after the words about eating what is set before you. This passage seems to prove conclusively that Thomas relies on our written gospels, at least in some measure, rather than on oral traditions.

A peculiar feature of Thomas's treatment of gospel sayings is his tendency to reverse their order. We have seen that the Naassenes too sometimes altered sequences when they quoted sayings—and in one instance where they quoted two separate gospel sayings, Thomas has an order the reverse of theirs! Such alterations of order are found in Sayings 22, 23, 48, 49, 76, 90, and 92. In most instances Thomas's changes can be explained as due to his desire to bring out more clearly the points he has in mind.[2]

The alterations do not help us to determine whether Thomas used oral traditions or written documents. It is possible that, as in the cases of the gospels of Matthew and Luke, the Gospel of Thomas is based partly on written materials and partly on oral traditions.

More important than the form, written or oral, of the materials he used is the nature of those materials. The portrait of Jesus which he paints is quite different from the portraits found in our gospels. First of all, it is obviously different because it lacks the narrative framework, the story of God's work in Christ, which the gospels supply. There are no stories of Jesus's conception, birth, baptism, temptation, calling his disciples, healing and other miracles, transfiguration, journey to Jerusalem, cleansing of the temple, Last Supper, arrest, trial, crucifixion, or resurrection. Events, and the treatment of events as fulfilling

[2] See the Commentaries on these sayings.

Old Testament prophecy, have vanished. There is no real movement in the Gospel of Thomas. There is no real history; there is no real eschatology; there is no sin; and there is no forgiveness (except for blasphemy against the Father and the Son in Saying 45). Practically everything directly related to life in first-century Palestine is gone. To be sure, something like this has already happened in the Gospel of John; but there Jesus is still recognizably the person who chose disciples, worked miracles, had conflicts with real opponents, and was crucified and rose again.[3]

Many of Thomas's sayings are closely parallel to those found in Matthew, and a detailed comparison will reveal that most of the similarities are between Thomas and the "Sermon on the Mount" (Matthew 5–7) and the collection of parables in Matthew 13, though Thomas also picks up isolated sayings and parables from other sections. Even within the "Sermon on the Mount," however, he omits everything that has to do with moral conduct and the performance of good works. He is not concerned with what Christians do but with what they know. Similarly, when compared with Luke, Thomas is closest to the collections of sayings found in chapters 6, 11, and 12; and, oddly enough, he takes a saying (79) from the story of the Crucifixion, though he changes its meaning completely. There seem to be no parallels to Mark alone; most of the sayings found in Mark are in Matthew or Luke. The parallels to John consist exclusively of sayings like those found in chapters 4 (the woman at the well of Samaria; living water), 7 and 8 (controversies with the Jews over Jesus's relation to the Father), and 12–17 (the farewell discourses addressed only to the disciples). From these similarities and differences [4] we should incline to hold that Thomas

---

[3] If John used a "sayings-source," this would be closer to Thomas; but the existence of such a source has not been demonstrated.

[4] A detailed list of parallels is given on the following pages.

made use of our gospels, selecting from them what he liked. It is possible that he made use of traditions which underlie them, but if we assume that he wrote toward the middle of the second century (since there is no trace of his work before the beginning of the third), it is more likely that he relied chiefly on written documents.

Were we to claim that he relied directly on primitive oral traditions and nothing else, we should have to ask whether the portrait of Jesus which he supplies is authentic or not. In other words, is it as historically credible as the portraits painted by the Church's evangelists? To answer this question we must go on to analyze the theology of his book as a whole.

THOMAS AND THE GOSPELS

A. MATTHEW

MATTHEW	SAYING	MATTHEW	SAYING	MATTHEW	SAYING
5:3	55	10:25	69	13:47–48	7
6	70	26	4, 5	57	32
8	70	27	34	15:11	14
9	49, 103	34	16	13	41
10–11	70	37–38	56, 98	14	35
11	69	39	57	16:28	17
14	25, 33	11:7–8	78	18:3	21
15	34	11–12	15, 47	8–9	23
45	2	15	66	12–13	104
6:3	63	28–30	90	19	49
20	76	12:29	22, 36	20	31
22–23	25	31–32	45	19:30	3
25	37	34–35	46	20:26	11
7:3, 5	27	47–50	96	21:21	49, 103
6–8	92	13:3–8	8	33–42	66–67
14(?)	51	12	42	22:1–10	65
16–19	46	24–30	58	15–22	97
8:20	86	31–32	20	24:35	10, 108
9:14	101	33	93	42–43	22
16–17	48	43	64, 66	43–44	100
37	73	44	106	25:1–13	75
10:16	40	45–46	76		

B. LUKE

LUKE	SAYING	LUKE	SAYING	LUKE	SAYING
4:24	32	10:2	73	12:51-53	16
5:34-35	101	23-24	47	56-57	4
36-39	48	11:9-10	92	13:20-21	93
6:20	55	21-22	36	30	3
21	70	27-28	79	14:16-24	65
22	69	33	34	26	98
35	2	34	25	26-27	56
41-42	27	39-40	89	15:4-6	104
44-45	46	42-43	99	16:13	48
7:24-25	78	52-53	40	16	47
28	47	12:2	4, 5	17:20-21	52, 111
8:5-8	8	3	31, 34	21	2
8	7	13-14	72	34	61
15	4, 5	16-20	64	19:42, 44	52
20-21	96	22	37	20:9-17	66-67
9:20	12	33	76	20-26	97
27	17	33-39	22	21:33	10, 108
58	86	35-39	100	23:29	79
10:1, 8-9	14	49	9, 16		

C. JOHN

JOHN	SAYING	JOHN	SAYING	JOHN	SAYING
4:14	12, 105(?)	8:25	44, 91	14:5, 8	25
22-23	70	42, 55(?)	102	15:8	19
23-24	79	47	19	15	12
27(?)	112	52	19, 108	16:5	92
7:34, 36	39	12:32	112	17:16, 23-24	50
37-38	12, 105(?)	13:33	11		
8:12	77	36	25		

D. APOCRYPHAL GOSPELS

EGYPTIANS	23, 38, 62(?)
HEBREWS	1, 11(?), 101

B. THE THEOLOGY OF THOMAS

The first impression we gain from the Gospel of Thomas, and the impression its author intended us to gain, is that it is a collection of "secret words" which the risen Jesus spoke. Unlike the Church's gospels, used within the community but also available to outsiders, the Gospel of Thomas is truly "apocryphal," in the sense that "apocryphal" means not so much "spurious" as "hidden" or "concealed." Moreover, the words which Jesus speaks do not mean what they seem to mean. They are hidden words and they contain a hidden sense, available only to the Gnostic-minded reader who searches for this sense. By finding it he achieves knowledge, and by means of knowledge he attains immortality. He "will not taste death."

At this point we may add that no doubt a good deal of illumination of Thomas's secret meaning will be provided by some of the other Nag Hammadi documents, but since most of them have not been published, and are not likely to be published in the immediate future, the non-Gnostic reader must make the best sense he can by trying to treat the sayings in Thomas more or less systematically.

Like the Church's gospels, Thomas is a gospel about Jesus. It tells us of the Jesus who is unique and incomparable (Saying 12), who is the revealer who "stood in the midst of the world and . . . appeared to them in flesh" (29). His origin is hidden in the Father, for he himself is the "beginning" and the "end" (18). He was not born of woman (15 and 47); he simply "came" in order to reveal his secrets and to give unimaginable gifts (17). He is the light which is over everything; he is the All, from whom everything has gone forth and to whom everything has returned (77). He is everywhere—if men will only seek for him (77). In so far as he appeared in flesh, he has gone away (11); it is in this sense that even his disciples can seek for him but not find him (39).

To a greater extent than the Church's gospels, Thomas is a gospel about the disciples. They are those who are by origin from the kingdom (Saying 30), from the light above (51); since they originated from the place of light, they are the elect of the living Father (51). They are "light-men" or "luminous-men" (25). Their essence consists of soul or spirit, dwelling in the "poverty" of the body (30). But they can become rich (81 and 107) and reign (1) if—unlike Adam (85)—they come to recognize their true nature. They can enter the kingdom of the Father if they will seek in order to find (1 and 92); if they will know themselves (2); if they will know the All (68); if they will recognize the inner man (71). Indeed, the kingdom *is* the inner man, for it is within the disciples (2); it is also outside them (2 and 111), in the sense that it is everywhere.

The true disciples come to be like infants (Saying 3) or little children (21, 23, and 38). This means that they transcend the distinctions of sex (23 and 112). They will become "single ones" or brothers (26 and 27) with one another.[5] They will be a "living spirit" (112). Thus they will recognize themselves as sons of the living Father (2 and 38) and "sons of man" (103) like the Son of Man (86). They will not experience death (Preface, 18, and 19). Instead, they have within them "a movement and a rest" (51) provided by the Father, an inward rest (60 and 90) which is achieved by their seeking and finding (1 and 92).

Knowing themselves, they reject the world; everything earthly must be abandoned. The "world" is hostile to them; they are hostile to it.[6] Heaven and earth are merely transitory (Sayings 10 and 108). The whole history of the world is a story of error, or worse. At the beginning of human history, Adam was unworthy of Jesus's true disciples (85). The prophets are dead and irrelevant as far as Jesus's disciples are concerned (53), even though the prophets may serve as messengers of the kingdom (88). The Jews (44),

[5] Sayings 3, 10, 11, 23, 24, 31, 50, 75, 103.
[6] Sayings 21, 22, 28, 57, 80, 107.

including the Pharisees (99), are to be rejected. Above all, religious observances are to be avoided by the true disciples. Circumcision is pointless (54). Prayer and fasting (5, 14, and 101), almsgiving and dietary laws (5 and 14) and ritual washing (89) are all irrelevant. Fasting and Sabbath observance now have a meaning which is spiritual, not literal (28).

Alienation from the religious history of mankind involves alienation from family and surroundings. One's father and mother are to be hated (56, 96, and 98). Caesar is apparently inferior to God, and God to Jesus (97). Anything old is incompatible with the new awareness (48).

With this world view in mind, Thomas then presses into his service a good many parables of the kingdom, derived from the gospels and elsewhere; he takes isolated sayings of Jesus and hints that their true meaning is to be found in the context he has provided for them.

What are we to make of this context? Is it a representation of some true and original Christianity, distorted by the Church's evangelists, especially by the synoptists, though not so much by John? We can well imagine that a second-century Gnostic would give a wholeheartedly affirmative answer to such questions. He would argue that the real Jesus had secretly taught what we find in Thomas, while his memory had been corrupted by apostles or evangelists who were preaching to Jews. These apostles had been blind and hard of heart; they had been unable to recognize the novelty and the uniqueness of Jesus's message. Only after his resurrection could the message be comprehended by an apostle who was spiritually capable of understanding.

In addition, it can be said that a twentieth-century successor of the Gnostics might well find much of the Gospel of Thomas attractive. Thomas is silent about sin and forgiveness. He records no miracles or, indeed, deeds of Jesus. There are no embarrassing stories about demons and the exorcism of demons. The kingdom of God is almost entirely inward, unrelated to time or history. One need not love his enemies. In fact, there is practically nothing which a disciple need do. "Doing the Father's will" is mentioned (after the synoptic gospels) in Saying 96, but at other points it is left out or replaced by knowing oneself or the kingdom. Self-knowledge is all-important.

In this respect Thomas is not unlike the Gospel of John, in which the only positive duty of Jesus's disciples is to "love one another" (John 13:34). Indeed, it is not unlike the synoptic gospels, which insist that man's duty is to love God with all his might and to love his neighbor as himself (Matthew 22:37–39; Mark 12:29–31; Luke 10:27). And we must remember that one of the key sentences of Thomas and of the Naassenes is derived from Luke 17:21: "The kingdom of God is within you."

What we find in Thomas, however, is a warping of the lines laid down in our gospels. Most conspicuously, the warping takes place in the author's rejection of the meaningfulness of historical events. Just the fact that his gospel —like that compiled by Thomas Jefferson—consists of nothing but sayings means that he has substituted a kind of spiritual understanding for the gospel of Jesus. And in the sayings that have parallels with our gospels, the version of Thomas lacks the connection with the past which was given by references to the Old Testament, as well as an emphasis on the importance of the future which was given by Jesus's statements about things to come. He has made the kingdom almost exclusively present, while in our gospels it is partly present but will be fully realized only in the future. Such a doctrine is essentially Gnostic, not Christian.

Interestingly, some of the emphases to be found in Thomas are much like those found in the Gospel of John. We have already noticed one example. Another, more important parallel is to be found in John's picture of the kingdom of God. Though John rarely mentions it, he seems to regard it as already realized in the work of Jesus and in the union of his disciples with him and with the Father. Eternal life is something which is already present. "He who hears my word and believes Him who sent me has eternal life and does not come to judgment but has passed from death into life. . . . The hour comes and now is when the dead will hear the voice of the Son of God and those who hear will live" (5:24–25).

In the Gospel of John these words are followed by others which present a stronger emphasis on the future. "The hour comes when all those who are in the tombs will hear his voice and will come forth, those who have done good things to a resurrection of life, those who have done evil things to a resurrection of condemnation" (5:28–29). Rudolf Bultmann and others have argued that these verses, and others like them, are the work of an ecclesiastical redactor who interpolated a gospel originally semi-Gnostic so that it would be accepted by the Church. This redactor laid emphasis on good works; he held that "salvation is of the Jews" (4:22); he brought in allusions to the synoptic gospels and to the Old Testament. Whatever conclusion we may reach as to the correctness of Bultmann's theory, the fact remains that it was in the "redacted" form that John's gospel was accepted by the Church. The Church was not willing to isolate any one element in Jesus's teaching from the others. The Jesus whom the Church knew and worshiped was not the Jesus of Paul alone or of the synoptics alone or of John alone. The Church insisted on the reality of Jesus as both human and divine, of man as both body and soul or spirit, of human existence as lived in past, present, and future. The Church insisted on the reality of sin and of forgiveness, of nature and of grace.

This grasp of reality is precisely what is lacking in the

Gospel of Thomas. Thomas is delighted to tell parables from the synoptic tradition when they suit his purpose. Some of the synoptic parables, however, are conspicuous by their absence. Among them is the story of the laborers in the vineyard (Matthew 20:1–16), where we learn that God is not like a human employer; he gives payments in accordance with grace, not in accordance with merit. Another omitted parable is that of the Good Samaritan (Luke 10:30–37), which teaches that to be a neighbor means to assist anyone who needs assistance, without discrimination. The prodigal son, freely forgiven by his father (Luke 15:11–32), is also absent, as is the story of the rich man and the beggar Lazarus (Luke 16:19–31). The parable of the Pharisee and the Publican, in which the Publican prays only with the words, "God, be merciful to me a sinner" (Luke 18:10–14), could not be retained by those who in their way so much resembled the Pharisee.

These parables do not contain the fullness of the Christian religion. It cannot be denied, however, that without them, without other examples of the teaching they present, and without the stories of Jesus's works of grace, we have an inadequate and distorted presentation of Christianity. The religious realities which the Church proclaimed were ultimately perverted by the Gospel of Thomas. For this reason Thomas, along with other documents which purported to contain secret sayings of Jesus, was rejected by the Church.

Even though much of the Gospel of Thomas seems to come from a time well before the end of the second century, and though many of the sayings contained in it were perfectly acceptable, the setting in which its author placed these sayings meant that as a whole the document had to be condemned by those who were concerned with the Jesus who really lived and really died, who really established the Church in which his memory was preserved.

The Gospel of Thomas is largely based on the Church's gospels. While more of its materials come from Matthew and Luke than from John, its point of view is more like that of John. It goes far beyond John, however, because its contents have been immersed in Gnosticism; it first emerges as a sacred writing of the Naassenes. Originally it may have been a kind of harmony of sayings of Jesus, some of a semi-Gnostic type. By the end of the second century, however, it had been taken over by the Gnostics and edited to suit their purposes.

The Jesus of the Gospel of Thomas is obviously related to the Jesus of the canonical gospels, but he has been transformed into the Gnostic revealer of secret wisdom and saving truth.

VIII

THE GOSPEL OF THOMAS
TRANSLATION
AND COMMENTARY

The Commentary is written with two aims in view: first, to try to explain what various sayings mean in the context of the Gospel of Thomas itself; second, to try to discover where they came from, at least in instances where their origins seem to be traceable, and to see what alterations have been made in the course of transmission or editing. We shall not consider later Gnostic or Manichaean texts in which the influence of Thomas is probably or certainly present.[1]

[PREFACE] (80.1–5)[2]

These are the secret words which Jesus the Living spoke and (which) Didymus Judas Thomas wrote. And He said: He who will find the interpretation of these words will not taste death

[1] For these matters, cf., Doresse, 119–205.
[2] The numbers in parentheses refer to the plate and line in the photographic edition of P. Labib, *Coptic Gnostic Papyri* I (Cairo, 1956). The

117

"Jesus the Living," who speaks the "secret words," is undoubtedly the risen Lord who, according to various Gnostic sects, gave detailed instruction to chosen individuals or small groups after his resurrection.

The Gnostics were not the only ones who attributed such sayings to Jesus. The Apocalypse of John begins with the words, "Revelation of Jesus Christ which God gave him to show to his servants, (concerning) what must take place immediately; and he indicated it by sending it through his angel to his servant John." Papias too (see page 30) reports what Jesus said to John alone. In addition, early Christian preachers were not averse to speaking in the person of Jesus. Toward the end of a sermon ascribed to Melito, bishop of Sardis about 170, we find these words:

He arose from the dead and thus cries to you:
> Who is he who contends against me (Isaiah 50:8)? Let him stand before me. I freed the condemned, I made the dead live again, I raise him who was buried. Who is he who raises his voice against me (cf., Isaiah 22:2)? I,

he says,
> the Christ, I am he who destroyed death and triumphed over the enemy and trod upon Hades and bound the strong one and brought men safely home to the heights of heaven, I,

he says,
> Christ . . . Therefore come hither, all ye families of men who are defiled with sins, and receive remission of sins. For I am your remission. I am the Passover of salvation, the lamb sacrificed for you. I am your ransom, I am your light, I am your savior, I am the resurrection, I am your king, I lead you up to the heights of heaven, I will show you the Father who is from the ages, I will raise you up by my right hand.

---

lines of plate 80 begin with the text of the Gospel of Thomas, not at the top of the page. The enumeration of the sayings is that of J. Leipoldt, *TLZ* 83 (1958), 481-93. For the Preface and Sayings 1-6 cf., *Oxyrhynchus Papyri* IV, 654.

The content of this homily is not Gnostic, but the method is the same as theirs.

Their idea is also based on statements in the gospels which refer to Jesus's being "alone" with the disciples (Mark 4:10) and to his explaining the parables to them "privately" (Mark 4:34). Only Peter, James, John, and Andrew heard Jesus's detailed prediction of things to come (Mark 13:3). According to John 20:24–29, a resurrection appearance took place especially for the benefit of Thomas.

Those who find the interpretation of the words will not taste death. A prediction that "some of those standing here will not taste death until they see the kingdom of God, come in power" is reported in the synoptic gospels (Mark 9:1; Matthew 16:28 ["the Son of Man coming in his kingdom"]; Luke 9:28 ["the kingdom of God]); but Thomas changes the future coming of kingdom or Son of Man to a man's finding the interpretation. Salvation is the result not of a future act of God but of knowledge. His idea is more like that expressed in John 8:52: "If anyone keeps my word, he will never taste death."

[1] (80.5–10)

Jesus said: [3]
  Let him who seeks not cease in his seeking
      until he finds;
  and when he finds, he will be troubled,
  and if he is troubled, he will marvel,
  and will be a king over the All.

This saying describes the process of seeking and finding, and the consequences which will result from it. Through being troubled and marveling will come reigning, with

[3] We meet this formula in the Greek as "Jesus says."

Jesus, over the All. In Saying 77, Jesus himself is the All, but he is the All in the sense that the All has come from him and has returned to him; he gives the All to his disciples. They become rich through gnosis and then they become kings (Saying 81). We may compare the saying recorded in Luke 22:29–30: "I ordain a kingdom for you, as the Father ordained it for me, so that you may eat and drink at my table in my kingdom; and you will sit on thrones, judging the twelve tribes of Israel" (cf., Matthew 19:28; also Matthew 25:34: "Inherit the kingdom prepared for you from the creation of the world"). "Rest" is mentioned not in the Coptic text but in the Greek fragment; but "rest" or "repose" occurs in Sayings 51, 52, 60, 61, 86, and 90. It is found in the Gospel of the Hebrews (Clement of Alexandria, *Strom.*, 2, 45, 5; 5, 96, 3), from which this saying is taken; presumably the author of Thomas changed the saying in order to lay emphasis on the idea of becoming a king. Compare 2 Timothy 2:11–12: "Trustworthy is the saying, 'If we have died with him, we shall also live with him; if we have endured, we shall reign with him." The difference, once more, is between the action of the Christian and the knowing of the Gnostic.

[2] (80.10–81.5)

Jesus said:
    If those who draw you say to you,
        Lo, the kingdom is in heaven,
            then the birds of heaven will precede you.
    If they say to you,
        It is in the sea,
            then the fish [4] *will precede you.*
    But the kingdom is within you and outside
        you.

When you know yourselves, then you will be
  known;
and you will know that you are the sons of the
  living Father.
But if you do not know yourselves,
  then you are in poverty,
  and you are poverty.

The kingdom is not in heaven (i.e., in the sky), nor is it
in the sea. It has no specific location. Similarly, Matthew
24:26–27 says that it is not in the desert or in the inner
chambers of a house (he mentions "eagles" in verse 28).
Thomas is close to the thought of Luke 17:21: "They will
not say, 'Lo, here' or 'There,' for behold, the kingdom of
God is within you." The Greek version of Thomas says that
the kingdom is within; the Coptic adds that it is also outside, perhaps because the Naassenes spoke of the kingdom
as "hidden and manifest at the same time." According to
Saying 111, the kingdom "is spread out upon the earth,
and men do not see it." It should be noted that Thomas
does not speak of "the kingdom of God." Indeed, "God" is
mentioned only in Saying 97, where he is evidently subordinated to Jesus ("gods" occurs in Saying 31). Wherever
the synoptic parallels speak of God, Thomas deletes the
word or substitutes "heaven" or "the Father" or "my
Father." Like other Gnostics, he prefers not to use the
ordinary term "God"; he may be reserving it for use as the
name of an inferior power.

The kingdom within is the equivalent of self-knowledge.
"When you know yourselves, then you will be known."
This reminds us of Paul's expression, "Now knowing God,
or rather having been known by God" (Galatians 4:9),
and, "Then I shall know, just as I have been known" (1
Corinthians 13:12). The Gnostic emphasis is different,

4 The Greek adds "of the sea."

however. For Paul, God now knows men; they will know him in the eschatological future. The Gnostic lays stress on knowing the self in order to be known, and his idea of knowing the self is an old Greek notion, expressed, for example, by the Delphic oracle; it is not characteristically Christian. The Gnostics will know that they are sons of the living Father; Christians will "become" sons of their Father in heaven (Matthew 5:45) or of the Most High (Luke 6:35)—and they will do so by loving their enemies, not by knowing.

The Gnostic says that self-knowledge results in freedom from poverty, rather in the way that Paul speaks of slavery to "poverty-stricken" celestial spirits as having been ended by Christ (Galatians 4:3–10). Paul also says that Jesus, "though he was rich, became poor, so that you might be made rich by his poverty" (2 Corinthians 8:9). Once more, the Christian emphasis is on the action of God in Christ; the Gnostic emphasis is on man's knowledge, even though this knowledge comes from revelation. For wealth in poverty cf., Saying 30; for becoming rich, cf., 81 and 107.

The Naassenes laid stress on the kingdom within; cf., Hippolytus, *Ref.*, 5, 7, 20–21; 5, 8, 8.

[3] (81.5–10)

Jesus said:
>*The old man in his days will not hesitate*
>>*to ask an infant of seven days about the*
>>>*place of life,*
>>*and he will live.*
>*For many of the first will be last,*
>>*and they will become a single one.*

If knowledge about the "place of life" can be given to an old man by an infant, it is evident that the knowledge is not ordinary human wisdom but something derived from revelation. This saying is probably the Gnostic explanation of the words of Jesus in Mark 10:14–15: "Let the children come to me and do not hinder them, for of such is the kingdom of God; verily I say to you, whoever does not receive the kingdom of God as a child will not enter into it" (cf., Matthew 19:14; cf. also Matthew 11:25; Luke 10:21). A little farther on in both Mark and Matthew we find the words which Thomas has added to the statement about the old man and the infant. "Many who are first will be last" (Mark 10:31; Matthew 19:30; 20:16; and Luke 13:30). The Coptic version has omitted the words, found in the synoptic gospels and in the Greek Thomas, "and the last, first." These words are necessary in order to lead to the conclusion, "And they will become a single one." Those who have been last will become first and will be united in the unity which means transcending differences of age and of sex (cf., Sayings 10, 16, 24, 49, 50, 75, 103, 112). It means returning to the original unity of creation (if one can speak of creation in a Gnostic system).

A saying vaguely resembling this one is quoted from the Gospel of Thomas by the Naassenes; cf., Hippolytus, *Ref.*, 5, 7, 20, and page 84 above.

[4] (81.10–14)

Jesus said:
  Know what is before your face,
  and what is hidden from you will be revealed
    to you;
  for there is nothing hidden which will not be
    manifest.

Recognition of revelation begins with knowing what is present. In Luke 12:57, Jesus asks his hearers why they

cannot of themselves judge what is right. By starting
with this ordinary knowledge (perhaps for Thomas a form
of self-knowledge; see Saying 2), one prepares himself for
revealed knowledge. "There is nothing hidden which will
not be manifest"—this saying occurs in Matthew 10:26;
Mark 4:22; and Luke 8:17; 12:2 (see Saying 5). Gnosis, in
Thomas, will reveal all secrets; "the beginning of perfection
is the knowledge of Man; complete perfection is the knowledge of God" (Hippolytus, *Ref.*, 5, 6, 6).

[5] (81.14–23)

His disciples asked him and said to him:
    Do you want us to fast?
    and in what way shall we pray
    and give alms?
    and what observances shall we keep in eating?
Jesus said:
    Do not speak falsely,
    and what you hate, do not do.
    For all things are revealed before heaven.
    For there is nothing hidden which will not be
        manifest,
    and there is nothing which is covered which
        will remain
    without being uncovered.

In this saying the injunctions of Matthew 6:16 ("When
you fast"), 6:5 ("when you pray"), and 6:2 ("when you
give alms") are rejected (see Sayings 14 and 101), in
opposition also to Christian practice as reflected in 2
Clement 16:2, and to Jewish practice as well (Tobit 4:7–
11; 12:8–9; Proverbs 10:2). Dietary laws are also can-
celed. There is a slight difference between the Greek,
where the mention of fasting, prayer, and almsgiving is
introduced in each case by the expression, "How shall

we . . . ?" and the Coptic, which begins, "Do you want us to fast?" The Coptic is simply making the meaning of the Greek more explicit. The reply ascribed to Jesus begins with counsel taken from Tobit. "Do not speak falsely, and what you hate, do not do" (Tobit 4:6, 15). Tobit had "do not do to another," but the Gnostic is concerned not with others but with himself. Since "all things are revealed before heaven" (the Father), religious observances make no difference. It is the inner disposition which counts. In the teaching of Jesus the inner disposition is certainly important, but outward observance is not rejected. Both factors are taken into account.

Thomas goes on to repeat the words with which Saying 4 had ended (see Commentary there) and he also repeats their sense in a different form: "There is nothing which is covered which will remain without being uncovered." This example of parallelism occurs in the Greek fragments, not at this point, but at the end of Saying 4, where it reads, "nothing buried which"—and then a break in the papyrus. Puech has filled in the missing words from a fifth- or sixth-century shroud inscription from Oxyrhynchus (see page 70), which reads, "There is nothing buried which will not be raised." But it seems hard to believe that this is the sense here, where—as in the rest of Thomas—there is no mention of resurrection. Perhaps one might regard the inscription as an orthodox, or semi-orthodox, revision of the saying in Thomas.

[6] (81.23–28)

Jesus said:
Blessed is the lion which man will eat,
that the lion may become a man;
and cursed is the man whom the lion will eat,
that the lion will become a man.

This saying, as Doresse notes (page 134), is extremely obscure. From other sayings in Thomas we may infer that the lion can be eaten only if it is killed and becomes a corpse (60), and that knowing the world is equivalent to finding a corpse (57)—the world is not worthy of those who find such a corpse. The Gnostic who has eaten what is dead has made it living (Saying 10). Therefore, by eating the dead lion, which may be the hostile world (cf., 1 Peter 5:8: "Your adversary the devil, like a raging lion . . ."), you can overcome the world by assimilating it to yourself. If the true inner man is consumed by the lion, and the lion becomes the man, the world has overcome the Gnostic (cf., Clement, *Excerpta ex Theodoto*, 84).

There is, of course, no parallel to this saying in the canonical gospels; the lion is a symbol of sexual desire in the Naassene system (Hippolytus, *Ref.*, 5, 8, 15).

[7] (81.28–82.3)

And he said:

> *Man is like a wise fisherman, who cast his net*
> *in the sea*
> > *and drew it out of the sea when it was full*
> > *of little fishes.*
> *Among them the wise fisherman found a large*
> *good fish.*
> *He cast all the little fishes down into the sea.*
> *He selected the large fish without difficulty.*
> *He who has ears to hear, let him hear.*

We should expect to read that "the kingdom" is like a fisherman (cf., Sayings 20, 76, 93–95, 104, 106); but for Thomas, true, inner man is *equivalent* to the kingdom. Moreover, Thomas sharply modifies the meaning of the parable in Matthew 13:47–48, on which he relies for some details. There the kingdom is like the net which brings in fish of all sorts, good and bad alike (a very un-Gnostic notion!). Thomas tells of the "experienced" fisherman who can select the best one of his catch (compare the "sheep" of Saying 104). The parable ends with the admonition, "He who has ears to hear, let him hear"; Matthew uses a similar admonition twice in the chapter in which he tells the parable of the dragnet (13:9, 43). Like Matthew, Thomas wants to show that there is a hidden meaning in the parable (see Sayings 22, 25, 64, 66, 93). The meaning is that only Gnostics are selected by Jesus or the Father, or that Gnostics select Christ.

[8] (82.3–13)

Jesus said:
   Behold, the sower went forth.
   He filled his hand; he threw.
   Some fell upon the road.
   The birds came (and) gathered them.
   Others fell upon the rock,
   and sent no root down into the earth
   and put forth no ear up to heaven.
   And others fell upon the thorns.
   They choked the seed
   and the worm ate them.
   And others fell upon the good earth
   and brought forth gooa fruit up to heaven.
   At times it came as sixty and at times as one
      hundred and twenty.

The parable of the sower is also related in the synoptic gospels (Matthew 13:3–8; Mark 4:3–8; Luke 8:5–8); in all three it ends with the admonition to "hear" which Thomas has placed at the end of Saying 7. Thomas adds a few details. The sower "filled his hand" before he cast the seed; this looks like no more than an attempt to indicate the fullness or completeness of the sowing (of souls or spirits). But when we read that the seed which fell on "the rock" (so only Luke) not only had no root but also "put forth no ear up to heaven" we are confronting a combination of this parable with the Naassene doctrine of the heavenward ascent of the good seed. The seed which fell upon thorns was not only choked but also eaten by the worm—presumably the worm of Gehenna (cf., Mark 9:48), though Thomas does not say so, since, like other Gnostics, he doubtless holds that hell is on earth. The good fruit, unlike the bad, is brought forth "up to heaven," sometimes sixty-fold, sometimes one-hundred-twenty-fold. Thomas feels free to give these figures since Matthew has one hundred, sixty, and thirty; Mark has thirty-sixty-one hundred; and Luke has simply one hundred. His figure is more logical; one hundred twenty is twice as much as sixty.

The Naassenes also quoted this parable and gave exegesis of it (see page 98); presumably Thomas, like them, referred it to the salvation of the true Gnostic by knowledge.

[9] (82.14–16)

Jesus said:
  I have cast a fire upon the world,
  and lo, I keep it until it burns up.

A similar saying in Luke 12:49 is clearly eschatological. "I came to cast fire on the earth, and how I wish that it were already kindled." Thomas changes future to past and present. The fire has been ignited, and Jesus keeps the world until it burns up; to be near the fire is to be near Jesus and the kingdom (Saying 82).

According to *Pistis Sophia* (chapter 141), the verse in Luke refers to the cleansing of the sins of the world by fire; elsewhere in the same work (chapter 116) the sins will be consumed by spiritual baptism.

[10] (82.16–25)

Jesus said:

This heaven will pass away,
and the one which is above it will pass away;
and that (plur.) *which is dead does not live,*
and that which lives will not die.

On the days when you were eating that
     (sing.) *which is dead,*
you were making it as that which lives.
When you (plural) *come into the light,*
what will you do?

Today you are as one;
you have both worked together.
But when you become two,
what will you do?

The first part of this saying is based on Matthew 24:35 (Mark 13:31; Luke 21:33): "The heaven and the earth will pass away, but my words [*logoi*] will not pass away." Thomas cannot believe that the synoptic saying can be as simple as it seems to be. He therefore takes "earth" to be a reference to another heaven above this one (early Christians sometimes spoke of a third heaven, as in 2 Corinthians 12:2, or of seven heavens), and interprets the *logoi* of Jesus as the true Gnostics, whom the Naassenes actually called "*logoi*." The dead world of matter has no life in it; the truly living ones, the Gnostics, will not die. Another version of this teaching is found in Saying 108.

The second part of the saying is paralleled by Naassene teaching reported by Hippolytus (*Ref.*, 5, 8, 32). Dead matter was made living when it was consumed by Gnostics; but when they come into the light, they no longer have anything to do with dead things; their true existence, no matter what it may seem to others, is purely spiritual. "Coming into the light" is Thomas's substitute for "eating living things" in Hippolytus's quotation; and eating living things means being spiritually fed by the pearls of the Father.

The third part of the saying describes the condition of the Gnostic believer. Those who were formerly divided have been united; they have worked together (Saying 59); they are at peace (49); they have become one (103). Unfortunately, it looks as if becoming "two" were regarded as the believer's goal. Perhaps it would be best to hold that the present unity of the believers represents their goal, and—in spite of the parallelism in the saying—that the becoming "two" is something they should avoid. Jesus is not a divider (Saying 72), except in the sense that he divides families into Gnostics and non-Gnostics (Saying 16).

[11] (82.25–30)

The disciples said to Jesus:
  We know that you will go away from us.
  Who will be great over us?
Jesus said to them:
  In the place to which you have gone,
  you will go to James the Just,
  for whose sake the heaven and the earth came
    into existence.

The disciples' question is based on words of disciples in the canonical gospels, though with considerable differences. In John 14:5 it is Thomas who says to Jesus, "Lord, we do not know where you are going," and in the synoptics the disciples discuss the question of who will be "greatest" or "first" among them (Matthew 18:1; 20:26; Mark 9:34; 10:43; Luke 9:46; 22:24); in several of these passages the discussion follows Jesus's prediction of his death and resurrection.

The answer which Jesus gives is again related to the conversation in the Gospel of John, where Jesus tells the disciples that he is going away to prepare a "place" for them (John 14:2–3). In Thomas, however, the "place" is apparently earthly rather than heavenly; it is a place in which they are to go to James the Just, "for whose sake the heaven and the earth came into existence." This exaltation of James is characteristic of Jewish-Christian and Naassene tradition (see pages 35, 86); it may be derived from the Gospel of the Hebrews. Doresse suggests (page 140) that James may here be regarded as a supernatural power, but there is nothing in Thomas which would favor such an interpretation.

[12] (82.30–83.7)

Jesus said to his disciples:
   Make comparisons; tell me what I am like.
Simon Peter said to him:
   You are like a just angel.
Matthew said to him:
   You are like a wise philosopher.
Thomas said to him:
   Master, my mouth will in no way endure
   my saying what you are like.
Jesus said:
   I am not your master,

since you drank (and) became drunk
from the bubbling spring
which I have distributed.

Jesus calls upon his disciples for something like a con-
fession of faith in him, as in the synoptic gospels he asks
them, "Who do men say . . . ?" and "Who do you say
that I am?" (Matthew 16:13–15; Mark 8:27–29; Luke
9:18–20.) Thomas does not believe that the essential
nature of Jesus can be expressed openly, or perhaps at
all, and therefore he insists that comparisons are being
used (cf., Mark 4:30: "How shall we compare the kingdom of God, or in what parable shall we put it?"). In the
synoptic passage it is Peter (Matthew has "Simon Peter")
who says that Jesus is the Christ—or, in an analogous
passage in John (6:68–69), that he is "the Holy One of
God," who has "words of eternal life."

In the synoptics, various erroneous interpretations pre-
cede the correct one. Jesus is John the Baptist, or Elijah,
Jeremiah, or some other prophet risen again. So in Thomas,
Simon Peter wrongly compares Jesus with an angel (a
belief widespread in early Jewish Christianity) and Matthew wrongly compares him with a wise philosopher.
Thomas rightly says that to compare Jesus with anything
is impossible; but as he does so, he addresses him as "Master." Thomas, like the man in Mark 10:17 (cf., Luke 18:18)
who calls Jesus "Good Master," is rebuked because of the
title he uses. Because he is a disciple of Jesus, he is not
a slave but a friend, for Jesus has made known everything
which he heard from his Father (John 15:15). The idea
expressed in Thomas is quite similar to that found in
John. Jesus is not Thomas's master because Thomas has
drunk from the bubbling spring which Jesus has distributed. This thought too is Johannine in origin. "The
water which I will give him will become in him a spring

of water bubbling up to eternal life" (John 4:14; cf., 7:37–38). "Drinking from the mouth of Jesus" is also mentioned in Saying 105; see Commentary there.

[13] (83.7–14)

And he took him, went aside (and) said to him
*   three words.*
But when Thomas came to his companions, they
*   asked him:*
*   What did Jesus say to you?*
Thomas said to them:
*   If I tell you one of the words he said to me,*
*   you will bring stones and you will cast them*
*   at me,*
*   and a fire will go forth from the stones and*
*   destroy you.*

Saying 13 is a continuation of the scene described in Saying 12. Jesus takes Thomas aside, as he takes other disciples aside in the canonical gospels, and speaks three secret words to him; Thomas refuses to repeat these to the other disciples, who would cast stones at him were he to express them (presumably because they would consider them blasphemous; the Hebrew penalty for blasphemy, i.e., naming the secret name of God, was stoning). The three words could, as Puech suggests (CRAcInscr, 1957, 156), be the names "Father, Son, and Holy Spirit" (as in a Coptic fragment of the Gospel of Bartholomew). Only blasphemy against the Holy Spirit is unforgivable, however (Saying 45). And the words must somehow be related to the fire which secretly penetrates the universe (see Commentary on Saying 9), for it will come out of the stones and consume the enemies of Thomas (for this use of fire, cf., Luke 9:54). We conclude that the words are probably the secret words of the Naassenes: *Caulacau, Saulasau, Zeesar* (Isaiah 28:10; Hippolytus, *Ref.*, 5, 8, 5); according to the Basilidians, Jesus "descended in the name Caulacau" (Irenaeus, *Adv. haer.*, 1, 24, 6). It is his secret Gnostic name which he is revealing to Thomas.

[14] (83.14–27)

Jesus said to them:
 If you fast, you will beget for yourselves a sin,
 and if you pray, you will be condemned,
 and if you give alms, you will do harm
  to your spirits.
 And if you go into every land, and travel in
  the regions,
 if they receive you,
 eat what they set before you.
 Heal the sick among them.
 For that which goes into your mouth
  will not defile you;
 but that which goes out of your mouth,
  that will defile you.

This saying deals with subjects already brought up in Saying 5: fasting, prayer, almsgiving, and dietary observances. Here the statements ascribed to Jesus are more explicit than they were before. Fasting produces sin; prayer results in condemnation; almsgiving harms the spirit. Some ground for Thomas's notion is given in Mark 2:18–20 (Matthew 9:14–15; Luke 5:33–35), where Jesus says that the sons of the bridechamber cannot fast while he is with them. Since Thomas regards the kingdom as present rather than future, fasting (a fortiori, prayer, almsgiving, and dietary laws) is pointless and, indeed, sinful. In order to reject the observance of dietary laws he turns to Luke 10:1–9 and quotes verses referring not only to going out into every land and to eating what is set before one but also to healing the sick. This mention of healing is irrelevant, since he then quotes Matthew 15:11 (cf., 15:17–18; Mark 7:18–20) on defilement as something internal rather than external. The saying seems to prove that Thomas used our gospels; see pages 105–6. Prayer and fasting are mentioned again in Saying 101.

[15] (83.27–31)

Jesus said:
When you see the one who was not born of
woman,
cast yourselves down on your faces,
and worship him; He is your Father.

Man who is born of woman is subject to sin, according to Job 14:1, as Doresse notes (page 143). The greatest of those born of women was John the Baptist (Matthew 11:11; Luke 7:28). Therefore, for our Gnostic (as for other Gnostics), Jesus cannot have been born of a woman (in spite of the fact that Paul says he was—Galatians 4:4). Of course it is possible that like some Gnostic teachers he held that while Jesus was born of a woman, the spiritual Christ descended upon him at the time of his baptism; the Naassenes believed that the threefold being descended upon Jesus. In any event, the one not born of woman is to be worshiped, since he is the (heavenly) Father. This conclusion seems to reflect the words of John 14:9: "He who has seen me has seen the Father" (cf., John 10:30: "I and the Father are one").

135

[16] (83.31–84.5)

Jesus said:
   Perhaps men think that I came
   to cast peace on the world;
   and they do not know that I came
   to cast division upon the earth,
   fire, sword, war.
   For five will be in a house;
   there will be three against two and two against
      three,
   the father against the son and the son against
      the father.
   And they will stand because they are single
      ones.

This saying is surprising when compared with the others which speak of peace and unity, for here Jesus plainly speaks of himself as a "divider." The two ideas can be reconciled, however, for peace and unity are characteristic of believers, Gnostic or Christian, while the division is that which comes into existence between them and outsiders. The saying is based on Luke 12:51–53 (Matthew 10:34); Luke 12:49 has already been paraphrased in Saying 9. "Perhaps men think" is derived from Luke's question, "Do you suppose . . . ?" "I came to cast peace" comes from Matthew, while "I came to cast division" is composed by the author of Thomas as a parallel to the preceding line, and to Luke 12:49, from which he derives the mention of "fire" ("sword" comes from Matthew). The next sentence is an almost exact quotation of Luke 12:52–53, though references to divisions among women are omitted because "women are not worthy of life" (Saying 112). Those who "stand" (and will not taste death, cf., Saying 18 and Commentary) are those who have broken their ties with earthly families and are "single ones" (cf., Sayings 50 and 75). They must hate father, mother, brothers, and sisters (Sayings 56 and 98).

The mention of "five" may possibly suggest to a Gnostic exegete that Jesus is speaking of the five senses, since sight, hearing, and touch are mentioned in the next saying. If this is so—and it is only a possibility—the two "good" senses might be sight and hearing, while the more "material" senses of taste, touch, and smell might be condemned.

[17] (84.5-9)

Jesus said:
  I will give you
  what eye has not seen
  and ear has not heard
  and hand has not touched
  and which has not come into the heart of man.

The apostle Paul quotes something very close to this saying, perhaps from a lost document, in 1 Corinthians 2:9: "As it is written, What eye has not seen and ear has not heard, and what has not entered into the heart of man, such things God has prepared for those who love him." By the end of the second century these words were ascribed to Jesus, as in the Martyrdom of Peter (chapter 10) and the Acts of Peter with Simon (chapter 39). Thomas adds a unique reference to the sense of touch. The joys of the kingdom are completely unrelated to sense perception. (We should add that, like other Gnostics, he undoubtedly rejected the accounts in the gospels which speak of Jesus's risen body as tangible—Luke 24:39; John 20:27). His phrasing of this saying is the exact reverse of 1 John 1:1, which speaks of "What we have heard, what we have seen with our eyes, what we beheld and our hands handled."

[18] (84.9–17)

The disciples said to Jesus:
  Tell us in what way our end will take place.
Jesus said:
  You have indeed uncovered the beginning
  so that you may seek the end;
  for in the place where the beginning is,
  there the end will be.
  Blessed is he who will stand in the beginning,
  and will know the end and will not taste death.

As in other sayings (38, 52, 111), the disciples of Jesus ask him about the coming of the kingdom or the new age, just as in the synoptic gospels (Matthew 24:3; Mark 13:4; Luke 21:7) they ask him, "When will these things be?" Matthew (24:36) and Mark (13:32) state that "not even the Son" knows about the day or the hour; but no Gnostic writer would reproduce this answer. Thomas says that the disciples have "uncovered" the beginning—presumably Jesus himself, as in much second-century theology and in patristic exegesis of John 8:25 (cf., Revelation 21:6: "I am the Alpha and the Omega, the beginning and the end"). The one who stands (in the beginning, one with Jesus, and knows the end) will not taste death (perhaps a paraphrase of Matthew 16:28; Mark 9:1; Luke 9:27) (cf., John 8:52 and Sayings 16 and 19).

[19] (84.17–25)

Jesus said:
  Blessed is he who was before he became.
  If you are my disciples and hear my words,
  these stones will serve you.

For you have five trees in paradise;
they do not stir, summer or winter,
and their leaves do not fall off.
He who will understand them will not taste
death.

The fourth-century apologist Lactantius treats the first
sentence of this saying as a prophecy uttered by Jeremiah
(*Div. inst.*, 4, 8); in the *Epideixis* (43) of Irenaeus, however, it is ascribed to Jesus (cf., J. P. Smith, *St. Irenaeus:*
Proof of the Apostolic Preaching, page 182, note 207).
Like Jesus, who "was" (John 1:1–2) before he "became"
incarnate (John 1:14), his disciples, who hear his words
because they themselves are "of God" (John 8:47), remain in him and have his words remaining in them; therefore whatever they ask will take place for them (John
15:8). Stones can become bread (Matthew 3:3; Luke 3:3),
or fire can come out of stones (Saying 13). Thomas
probably has in mind the creation of food out of stones
(cf. also Matthew 7:9: "What man of you, if his son asks
him for bread—will he give him a stone?"), for he goes on
to speak of the five never-failing trees in paradise. These
trees, mentioned in *Pistis Sophia* (chapters 1 and elsewhere) and among the Manichees, are probably trees
which give spiritual sustenance to the five spiritual senses.
They are trees of life like the single one mentioned in
Revelation 22:2 (cf., the Gospel of Eve[?] in Epiphanius,
Pan., 26, 5). They must be spiritual, since Thomas says
that "he who will understand them will not taste death."
To understand them is thus equivalent to "keeping the
word" of Jesus (John 8:52).

[20] (84.26–33)

The disciples said to Jesus:
Tell us what the kingdom of heaven is like.

He said to them:
> *It is like a grain of mustard, smaller than all*
> *the seeds.*
> *But when it falls on the earth which is tilled,*
> *it sends forth a great branch and becomes a*
> *covering*
> *for the birds of heaven.*

As in the Gospel of John (16:12), Jesus tells his dsciples that he has much more to say, but that they cannot bear it now, so in Thomas the disciples turn from the secret teaching about paradise to ask what the kingdom is like. Jesus replies with a parable derived from the synoptic tradition (Matthew 13:31–32; Mark 4:30–32; Luke 13:18–19). Only in Mark does a question (asked by Jesus himself) introduce the parable; only in Matthew is the kingdom called "of heaven" or do we find the words, "but when." None of the gospels say that the ground has been tilled, but Thomas is indicating that only the soil of true Gnostics is ready to receive the mustard seed. The tree naturally covers the birds which, according to the gospels, dwell in it, though in Thomas's mind it may also conceal them. The main emphasis of the parable in Thomas, however, as in the gospels, is on the infinitesimal size of the seed (as in Naassene exegesis, Hippolytus, *Ref.*, 5, 9, 6).

[21]   (84.33–85.6)

Mariham said to Jesus:
> *What are your disciples like?*
He said:
> *They are like little children*
> *who dwell in a field which is not theirs.*
> *When the masters of the field come,*
> *they will say, Leave our field to us!*

They are naked before their eyes,
as they leave it to them and give them their
field.

Here Mariham (the Mariamme of the Naassenes—Hippolytus, *Ref.*, 5, 7, 1—also mentioned in Saying 112), asks
a question and is told that the disciples are "like little
children" (Matthew 18:3; cf., 1 Corinthians 14:20). The
children live in an alien field, which must be the world, as
in Matthew 13:38. "Leave our field to us!" recalls the
command of the farmer in Matthew 13:30: "Leave both to
grow up together until the harvest." Moreover, in Matthew
24:40–42 there are mysterious references to "two in a
field," to one's being left, and to the coming of a master.
Whatever synoptic reminiscences there may be, these
have been subordinated to the notion of being naked
(see Saying 38). The true Gnostic wants to strip off the
body (contrast 2 Corinthians 5:4: "not to be stripped but
to be clad upon") and leave the world.

[22] (85.6–19)

Therefore I say:
If the householder knows that the thief is
coming,
he will watch before he comes
and will not let him dig into his house of his
kingdom
to carry off his vessels.
But you, be watchful over against the world.
Gird your loins
with a great power
so that no robber may find a way
to come to you.

> For the (fulfillment of your) need, which you
>   await,
> will be found.
> May there be an understanding man in your
>   midst!
> After the fruit ripened,
> he came in haste with his sickle in his hand
> (and) reaped.
> He who has ears to hear, let him hear!

This saying is a continuation of the previous one. Jesus tells the disciples a parable found in Luke 12:39 and Matthew 24:43 (the words "to carry off his vessels" are added from Matthew 12:29; Mark 3:27; see Saying 36). As in Matthew 24:42, an admonition to "watch" is combined with the parable. Thomas has changed its meaning, however. In the gospels the parable pointed toward the future coming of the kingdom; Thomas deletes the words "at what hour." He introduces a static, Gnostic conception by identifying the "house" with the "kingdom," and states that the watchfulness is to be "over against the world."

From the same context in Luke (as in Saying 100) comes the counsel, "Gird your loins!" Thomas explains that this means to gird yourself with "a great power" (the power of the kingdom) so that no robber may come to you (Luke 12:33). You will be given what you need (Luke 12:22–32). An "understanding man" is mentioned in Luke 12:42. Because of such parallels, it is hard to believe that Thomas is doing anything but creating a mosaic of sayings chiefly derived from Luke.

The reaper reminds us of John the Baptist as described in Matthew 3:12 and Luke 3:17, but it is not clear who is meant in Thomas. The presence of a hidden meaning is indicated by the final admonition to "hear."

[23] (85.20–35)

Jesus saw little ones receiving milk.
He said to his disciples:
  These little ones receiving milk
  are like those who enter into the kingdom.
They said to him:
  If we are little ones,
  will we enter into the kingdom?
Jesus said to them:
  When you make the two one,
  and make the inside like the outside,
  and the outside like the inside,
  and the upper side like the under side,
  and (in such a way) that you make the man
      (with) the woman a single one,
  in order that the man is not man and the
      woman is not woman;
  when you make eyes in place of an eye,
  and a hand in place of a hand,
  and a foot in place of a foot,
  an image in place of an image;
  then you will go into [the kingdom].

Infants (as in Sayings 3, 21, and 38) may be compared with those who enter into the kingdom (cf., John 3, 3.5). But entering the kingdom means more than becoming childlike. The two must become one; all earthly differences must be obliterated, including—especially—those of sex. Sayings very much like this one are preserved in the Gospel of the Egyptians, in 2 Clement 12:2, and in the Martyrdom of Peter (see pages 78–79). The unity of Christian believers in the body of Christ is, of course, based on the New Testament. Doresse (pages 155–56) cites John 17:11; 20–23; Romans 12:4–5; 1 Corinthians 12:27; Ephesians 2:14–18; and he points out that in Ephesians 5:32 the unity of Adam and Eve (i.e., of human marriage) is referred to "Christ and the Church." It is perhaps more important to notice that in Galatians 3:28 Paul says that "there is neither Jew nor Greek, neither slave nor free men, *neither male nor female; for you are all one in Christ Jesus.*" This kind of unity looks back to the first creation story in Genesis, where "man" is male and female; it is the second creation story which sharply differentiates Eve from Adam. The original state of creation is to be reached through spiritual union. Man is not to be man; woman is not to be woman (though according to Saying 112 she is to become man—i.e., fully human in a spiritual sense).

This doctrine was also expressed by the Naassenes, who held that the primal man was androgynous and therefore rejected sexual intercourse (Hippolytus, *Ref.*, 5, 7, 14), since it leads to death (*Ref.*, 5, 7, 39); all Gnostics become bridegrooms, "having been made male through the virginal Spirit" (*Ref.*, 5, 8, 44).

The Gnostic, who is a eunuch for the sake of the kingdom (Matthew 19:12), plucks out his eye and cuts off his foot and his hand (Matthew 18:9–8; Mark 9:47; 44; 45). By so doing, he gains a spiritual member (cf., "an eye for an eye," Matthew 5:38) and enters into the kingdom. "Eye" is mentioned first because it is found first in Matthew 5:28–30, a condemnation of lust which the Gnostics understood as condemning sexual desire in general.

[24] (86.1–3)

Jesus said:
I will choose you,
one from a thousand and two from ten thousand,

*and they will stand because they are a single
one.*

The expression "One from a thousand" comes from Ecclesiastes 7:28, where it refers to the proportion of good
men to men in general. As developed into a Gnostic slogan,
it was quoted by the Basilidians (see page 83) and in
Pistis Sophia (chapter 134). In the Basilidians' view, they
alone were men. For Thomas, the one will stand because
he is one, and the two, because the two become one (in
the Gnostic community; see Commentary on Saying 23).

[25] (86.3–10)

His disciples said:
Show us the place where you are,
for it is necessary for us to seek it.
He said to them:
He who has ears, let him hear!
There is light within a light-man
and it illuminates the whole world;
if it does not illuminate it, (it is) darkness.

The disciples ask to be shown where Jesus is, just as
in John 13:36 Simon Peter asks where he is going, in John
14:5 Thomas asks about the way, and in John 14:8 Philip
asks to be shown the Father. Jesus replies by urging them
to "hear" the hidden meaning of his words. They already
possess spiritual illumination within themselves, for they
have spiritual "eyes" (Saying 23). Thomas paraphrases a
saying of Jesus about the eye in Matthew 6:22–23; Luke
11:34–36. For the "luminous" body of the gospels he substitutes the Gnostic conception of the "luminous-man"
(*Pistis Sophia*, chapter 125). Their light illuminates the
whole world because they are "the light of the world"

(Matthew 5:14; another quotation of this verse is in Saying 33).

[26] (86.10–12)

Jesus said:
  Love your brother as your soul;
  keep him like the apple of your eye.

Here we have a Jewish proverbial expression, the first half of which comes from Leviticus 19:17–18. By "brother," however, Thomas means not an Israelite or another human being but another Gnostic. Contrast the New Testament teaching in general.

[27] (86.12–17)[5]

Jesus said:
  You see the splinter in your brother's eye;
  but you do not see the beam in your own eye.
  When you cast out the beam from your own
    eye,
  then you will see to cast out the splinter
    from your brother's eye.

The saying is very slightly modified from a saying related in Matthew 7:3, 5 and in Luke 6:41–42. In the Coptic version it leads without a break into Saying 28, and thus seems to imply that the beam in the Gnostic's eye is his absolute rejection of fasting and Sabbath observance. He ought to explain the spiritual meaning of these actions to his Jewish, or Jewish-Christian, brothers, or potential brothers.

[5] For Sayings 27–34 cf., P. Oxy. I, 1.

[28] (86.17–20)

⟨*Jesus said:*⟩
 If you do not fast to the world,
   you will not find the kingdom;
 if you do not truly keep the Sabbath,
   you will not see the Father.

The words of this saying were early circulated in the Church; fasting to the world is mentioned by Clement of Alexandria (*Strom.*, 3, 99, 4; *Ecl. proph.*, 14, 1), and (spiritually) keeping the Sabbath occurs in the writings of Justin (*Dial.*, 12, 3) and Tertullian (*Adv. Jud.*, 4). Gnostics, like other Christians, believed that the Old Testament ritual law now had a symbolic meaning.

[29] (86.20–31)

Jesus said:
 I stood in the midst of the world
   and I appeared to them in flesh;
 I found all of them drunken;
   I found none among them thirsty.
 And my soul was pained for the children of
   men,
   for they are blind in their hearts,
   and they do not see
   that they came empty into the world
   seeking also to leave the world empty.
 But now they are drunken.
 When they throw off their wine,
   then they will repent.

In the synoptic gospels Jesus expresses appeals not unlike this one; cf., Matthew 11:25–30; 23; 37; Luke 13:34.

Drunkenness is likened to ignorance of God in 1 Corinthians 15:34. In 1 Timothy 3:16 we read that "he was manifested in flesh." But as a whole this saying is closer to the description of the revealer given in the *Hermetica,* semi-Gnostic theosophical literature of the second or third century. The *Poimandres* (*Herm.,* 1, 27) contains a statement very much like this saying.

[30] (86.31–87.2)

Jesus said:
> *If the flesh came into existence for the sake of*
> *the spirit, (it is) a wonder;*
> *but if the spirit (came into existence) for the*
> *sake of the body,*
> *it is a wonder of [wonders];*
> *but I wonder at how [this] great wealth*
> *has dwelt in this poverty.*

The flesh did not come into existence for the spirit, for the two are opposed both in Pauline (Galatians 5:17; Romans 8:6, etc.) and in Gnostic thought. Similarly the spirit did not come into existence for the body. It is a miracle that great (spiritual) wealth (Saying 85) can dwell in poverty (cf., Saying 2 and Commentary). For the contrast of soul with body see Saying 87; for that of soul with flesh, Saying 110. For "wonder of wonders," see Hippolytus, *Ref.,* 5, 8, 18.

[31] (87.2–5)

Jesus said:
> *Where there are three gods,*
> *they are gods.*
> *Where there are two or one,*
> *I am with him.*[6]

[6] P. Oxy. I, 1 inserts the final section of Saying 77 at this point.

This saying is found in different versions, Greek and Coptic. The Greek speaks of some number of persons—more than one—who are not without God (if the fragmentary text has been correctly restored; perhaps it should read, "Wherever there are two, they *are* without God"), and goes on to say, "And where there is one alone, I say, I am with him." Then it adds the last section of Saying 77 (Coptic). The Coptic, on the other hand, says that three gods are gods, and that where there are two or one, Jesus is with him. The second half of the saying is fairly easy to explain. It looks like a Gnostic version of, "Where there are two or three gathered in my name, there am I in their midst" (Matthew 18:20); as a Gnostic, Thomas reduces the numbers. Which version is really the original can hardly be determined; the medieval Cathari seem to have quoted a combination of both versions. "Where there was one of his little ones, he would be with him; and where there were two, similarly; and where there were three, in the same way" (v. Döllinger, *Beiträge zur Sektengeschichte des Mittelalters,* II, page 210). The remark about the gods may possibly involve a criticism of Christian doctrine as tritheism; according to the Coptic text, Christians may be worshiping three (mere) gods (for "God" as possibly inferior to Jesus, see Saying 97).

[32] (87.5–7)

Jesus said:
No prophet is acceptable in his village;
no physician heals those who know him.

This is the first of a sequence of synoptic-type sayings (32–37), rather miscellaneous in character. This saying is derived from Luke 4:24, to which it is closer than to the parallels (Matthew 13:57; Mark 6:4). The second part of it has sometimes been regarded as authentic, but it may equally well be a modification of the "proverb" quoted in Luke 4:23: "Physician, heal yourself." As we shall see in dealing with the next saying, Thomas likes to expand synoptic sayings.

[33] (87.7–10)

Jesus said:
A city built on a high mountain (and)
    fortified
cannot fall and cannot remain hidden.

This saying is based on Matthew 5:14, but it has become mixed up with something else in the course of transmission. A city lying on a high mountain cannot be hidden (Matthew); a city which is fortified cannot fall. The first idea, like others used in parabolic sayings, is self-evident; the second is false.

[34] (87.10–18)

Jesus said:
What you hear in your ear
preach to another ear upon your roofs.
For no one lights a lamp and puts it under a
    bushel
and no one puts it in a hidden place;
but he puts it on the lamp stand,
so that all who go in and come out
may see its light.

Here we have nothing but a combination of sayings about an ear (Matthew 10:27; Luke 12:3; both sayings mention "light") and about lighting a lamp (Luke 11:33; 8:16; Matthew 5:15). "Lamp" and "ear" are also mentioned together in Mark 4:21–24, but presumably Saying 34 follows Saying 33 because of the sequence in Matthew 5:14–15; Thomas, or his source, then added Matthew 10:27; Luke 12:3.

[35] (87.18–20)

Jesus said:
 If a blind man leads a blind man,
 both fall down into a pit.

This saying is derived from Matthew 15:14; for its substance is presented as a question in Luke 6:39. It follows Saying 34, because the mention of "light" in that saying leads Thomas to think of sight or the lack of it.

[36] (87.20–24)

Jesus said:
 It is impossible for anyone to go
 into the house of the strong man,
 and to take it by force
 unless he binds his hands;
 then he will plunder his house.

Here is another synoptic parable, found in Matthew 12:29; Mark 3:27; and Luke 11:21–22. The beginning of the saying, "It is impossible," is close to Matthew and Mark, but the mention of "taking by force" recalls the "armor" of Luke. Thomas had already spoken of stealing "vessels" (mentioned by Matthew and Mark in this parable) in Saying 22; he therefore follows Luke's version here. The point of the parable is that Jesus has already overcome the world, and he has "bound the hands" of the strong man.

THE SECRET SAYINGS OF JESUS

[37] (87.24–27) [7]

Jesus said:
  Do not take care
    from morning to evening
    and from evening to morning
  what you will put on yourselves.[8]

Do not worry about what you will wear (Matthew
6:25; Luke 12:22). "Morning and evening" are presumably Thomas's' substitutes for "the morrow" of Matthew
6:34. In the Greek version more quotations from the gospels are provided (Matthew 6:25, 28, 27; Luke 12:22, 27,
25). This fact may suggest that the editor of Coptic
Thomas wanted to remove such obvious traces of his
sources.

[38] (87.27–88.2)

His disciples said:
  On what day will you appear to us,
  and on what day will we see you?
Jesus said:
  When you undress yourselves and are not
      ashamed,
  and take your clothing
  and lay them under your feet,
    like little children,
  and tread on them;
  then [you will become] sons of the Living One
  and you will have no fear.

---

[7] For Sayings 37–40 cf., P. Oxy. IV, 655.
[8] The Greek papyrus adds excerpts from Matthew 6:25, 28 and Luke
12:22, 27 at this point.

"On what day will you appear to us?" has the same meaning as, "On what day will the rest of the dead take place? And on what day does the new world come?" (Saying 52) and, "On what day does the kingdom come?" (Saying 111). Whereas in the Church's gospels such questions are not really answered, Thomas answers them by stating that the kingdom has come; it need only be recognized. Here the disciples are to become "naked" (Saying 21) by stripping off the body; they are to become "like little children." Such stripping is mentioned by the Naassenes (Hippolytus, *Ref.*, 5, 8, 44); while treading on the garment of shame was found in the Gospel of the Egyptians (Clement, *Strom.*, 3, 92, 2). The disciples will be "sons of the Living Father" (see Saying 2).

[39] (88.2–7)

Jesus said:
  Many times you have desired
  to hear these words which I speak to you,
  and you have no one else from whom to hear
    them.
  The days will come
    (when) you will seek me
    (and) you will not find me.

The second-century Marcosians, according to Irenaeus (*Adv. haer.*, 1, 20, 2), quoted this saying in a slightly different form. "Many times they desired to hear one of these words, and they had no one to tell them." The saying may be based on Luke 17:22: "The days will come when you desire to see one of the days of the Son of Man, and you will not see." As usual, Thomas—or a predecessor —changes what is future in the gospels to present and past. "The days will come" (Luke) when "you will seek me and will not find me" (John 7:34). Here the gospel picture of something future is retained, perhaps because in Gnosticism the eschatological emphasis of Christianity could not be entirely dropped.

[40] (88.7–13)

Jesus said:
The Pharisees and the scribes
received the keys of knowledge;
they hid them and did not enter in,
and did not permit those who wanted to
come in.
But you be wise as serpents
and sincere as doves.

Thomas has changed Jesus's address to the scribes (Luke 11:52–53) to a saying about the Pharisees and the scribes, who are often associated in the gospels. (The same thought is expressed in Saying 99.) In the presence of such enemies, the believers are to be wise as serpents (as in the Naassene system?) and sincere as doves (Matthew 10:16).

[41] (88.13–16)

Jesus said:
A vine was planted outside of the Father,
and it has not become strong;
it will be uprooted and it will perish.

Wise believers have an assurance like that given in Matthew 15:13: "Every plant which my heavenly Father did not plant will be uprooted." Similarly, according to John 15:6, branches of the vine (Jesus) which do not remain in him will wither and be burned up.

[42] (88.16–18)

Jesus said:
He who has (something) in his hand,
to him it will be given;
and he who has nothing,
from him even the little he has will be taken
away.

Rewards are given on the ground of what is already possessed. Thomas takes a saying used in the gospels, either in isolation (Mark 4:25; Luke 8:18), or as encouragement to understand parables (Matthew 13:12), or as the conclusion for a parable (Matthew 25:29; Luke 19:26), and sets it forth here. A more Gnostic version occurs in Saying 71.

[43] (88.19)

Jesus said:
Come into being as you pass away.

Presumably the saying has much the same meaning as Paul's words (2 Corinthians 4:16): "If our outer man is perishing, our inner man is renewed day by day."

[44] (88.20–26)

His disciples said to him:
Who are you that you say these things to us?
⟨*Jesus said:*⟩
In what I say to you, you do not understand
who I am.
But you have become like the Jews;
for they love the tree (and) hate its fruit,
and they love the fruit (and) hate the tree.

155

In this saying we have a highly artificial construction. It takes its point of departure from John 8:25, where the Jews ask Jesus who he is; they know neither him nor his Father (John 8:19). Thomas has transferred the question to the disciples so that Jesus can say that they are "like the Jews." The Jews do not understand that the nature of the tree is identical with that of the fruit (Matthew 7:16–20; Luke 6:43–44). And in both Matthew and Luke the discussion of trees and fruits is followed by a rebuke to those who call Jesus "Lord" but do not obey him. It looks as if Thomas has consciously tried to make his meaning more mysterious than that reflected in the gospels.

[45] (88.26–31)

Jesus said:
  He who blasphemes the Father
    will be forgiven,
  and he who blasphemes the Son
    will be forgiven,
  but he who blasphemes the Holy Spirit
    will not be forgiven,
  either on earth or in heaven.

Blasphemy against the Father is presumably included in the "every blasphemy" mentioned in the synoptic gospels (Matthew 12:31; Mark 3:28), and these gospels go on to state that blasphemy against the Son of Man is forgivable, while that against the Holy Spirit is not (also Luke 12:10). Thomas has changed "Son of Man" to "Son" (retained in Saying 86), and has changed Matthew's eschatological words, "in this age or in the one to come," to "either on earth or in heaven" (as in the Lord's Prayer, Matthew 6:10). The sequence Father-Son-Holy Spirit reflects Christian teaching (cf., Matthew 28:19).

[46] (88.31–89.6)

Jesus said:

Grapes are not gathered from thorns,
nor are figs plucked from camel's thorn.
They give no fruit.
And a good man brings forth good from his
*   treasure.*
A wicked man brings forth evil from his evil
*   treasure*
* which is in his heart,*
and says evil things;
for from the abundance of the heart he brings
*   forth evil things.*

From the fruits mentioned in Saying 44, Thomas goes on to give other sayings on the same subject, beginning with Matthew 7:16, then continuing with its parallel, Luke 6:44–45. Luke 6:45 is parallel to Matthew 12:35, which also puts the saying about "treasure" in the context of "saying things"; but the saying in Thomas can be explained as based simply on a combination of Matthew 7:16–19 with Luke 6:44–45. The Gnostic is presumably the one who brings forth good things.

[47] (89.6–12)

Jesus said:

From Adam to John the Baptist
no one born of women is greater than John the
*   Baptist*
so that his eyes will not . . .
But I said:
* He among you who will become a little one*
* will understand the kingdom*
* and will be greater than John.*

This saying is adapted from Matthew 11:11–12 (Luke 7:28), where we read that "No one has arisen, among those born of women, greater than John the Baptist; but the least [smallest] in the kingdom of heaven is greater than he"; the next saying begins with the words, "From the days of John the Baptist"—Thomas seems to have used these words as the model for his expression, "From Adam to John the Baptist." Thomas also changes "in the kingdom of heaven" to "will understand the kingdom." The words, "so that his eyes will not" (Doresse supplies "lose themselves") are incomprehensible.

[48] (89.12–23)

Jesus said:
> *It is impossible for a man to mount two horses and stretch two bows,*
> *and it is impossible for a slave to serve two masters.*
> *Either he will honor the one and despise the other,*
> *⟨or he will hate the one and love the other.⟩*
> *No one drinks old wine and immediately desires to drink new wine.*
> *And new wine is not put into old skins, lest they split.*
> *And old wine is not put into new skins, lest it perish.*
> *And old patch is not put on a new garment, since a rip will result.*

One must choose whether to follow Jesus and be in the kingdom or to go along with the world. Thomas adds two comparisons which have a proverbial ring to a collection of verses taken from the gospel of Luke. A slave cannot serve two masters (Luke 16:13; Matthew 6:24 is slightly different), and no one after drinking old wine wants new (Luke 3:39). New wine is not put in old skins (Luke 5:37); old wine is not put in new skins (not in the gospels, though "old wine" is mentioned in Luke 5:39). An old patch is not put on a new garment; here Thomas changes the thought from that of the new patch and the old garment (Luke 5:36; Matthew 9:16; Mark 2:21), presumably because he is thinking of life in the new world (Saying 52).

[49] (89.24–27)

Jesus said:
  If two make peace with one another in the
    same house,
  they will say to the mountain,
    Move! and it will move.

In form this saying is quite similar to Saying 103, where two, becoming one, become sons of men; they say, "Mountain, be removed!" and it moves. We should infer that making peace with one another is the same thing as becoming one, and it also means becoming "sons of men." Doresse (page 175) notes that the combination then resembles Matthew 5:9: "Blessed are the peacemakers, for they shall be called sons of God." (Thomas as usual removes a mention of God.) There is another way of viewing Saying 49 by itself. It clearly begins with something like Matthew 18:19 ("if two of you agree on earth"), and this verse is parallel to Mark 11:24; but the second part of the saying is parallel to the preceding verse in Mark. One must suppose either that the author of Thomas gave close study to gospel parallels, or that he relied on an earlier document in which the parallels had been combined—such as the *Diatessaron* of Tatian, probably written between 150 and 170.

[50] (89.27–30)

Jesus said:
  Blessed are the single ones and the elect,
    for you will find the kingdom.
  For you (are) from it,
    (and) you will enter into it again.

The "single" or "solitary" ones will find the kingdom or, in Saying 75, will enter the bridechamber. They are no more from the world than Jesus himself is (John 17:16); they are one as Jesus and the Father are one (John 17:23). Where Jesus is, they will also be (John 17:24).

[51] (89.30–90.7)

Jesus said:
  If they say to you, Whence have you come?
  say to them, We came from the light,
  the place where the light came into existence
    through itself alone;
    it has . . .
    . . . their image.
  If they say to you, (Who are) you?
  say, We are his sons, and we are
  the elect of the living Father.
  If they ask you, What is the sign of your
    Father who is within you?
  say to them, It is a movement and a rest.

This saying continues the thought of Saying 50. The disciples are the light of the world (Matthew 7:14) because Jesus is the light of the world (John 8:12). They

are from above, from the place where the light shines in
the darkness (John 1:5). They are sons of the light (?),
and the elect. If men ask for a sign, as they asked Jesus
(Mark 8:11–12; Matthew 16:1–4; Luke 11:16, 29–30), no
startling miracle can be shown them, but only "a movement and a rest." The "rest" must be the rest characteristic of the kingdom (Sayings 1 [Greek], 52, 90); the "movement" is ultimately that of the unmoved mover, according
to the Naassenes (Hippolytus, *Ref.*, 5, 7, 25).

[52] (90.7–12)

His disciples said to him:
  On what day will the rest of the dead take
    place?
  And on what day does the new world come?
He said to them:
  That (rest) for which you are waiting has
    come;
  but you do not recognize it.

This saying too looks like a continuation of what pre-
cedes it. The question is Thomas's equivalent for the
Pharisees' question about the coming of the kingdom in
Luke 17:20; the answer is like the answer in Luke 17:21:
"The kingdom of God is within you." Because, like the
earthly Jerusalem (Luke 19:42, 44), the disciples are still
blind, they do not (fully) recognize its presence—in Jesus.
See Sayings 2 and 111.

[53] (90.12–18)

His disciples said to him:
  Twenty-four prophets spoke in Israel,
  and all of them spoke concerning you.

He said to them:
You have abandoned the one who lives before
your eyes,
and you have spoken concerning the dead.

The disciples are still concerned with the fulfillment of prophecy; they are thinking about the twenty-four Jewish prophets. (In the old Jewish *Lives of the Prophets* (edited by C. C. Torrey, Philadelphia, 1946) only twenty-three prophets are mentioned, but Thomas reaches twenty-four by adding John the Baptist.) Thomas is not interested in prophecy or its fulfillment; prophets are mentioned elsewhere only in Saying 88, as coming to believers and asking them for what they have; and Old Testament references in the teaching of Jesus are omitted (see, for example, Saying 66 and Commentary). So Jesus rebukes the disciples for this concern. "You have left the one who lives before your eyes and you have spoken concerning the dead." This saying is quoted, from the "apocryphal writings" of heretics (perhaps Marcionites, who, like Thomas, rejected the Old Testament) by Augustine; see page 90.

[54] (90.18–23)

His disciples said to him:
Is circumcision profitable or not?
He said to them:
If it were profitable, their father
would have begotten them circumcised
from their mother.
But the true circumcision in the Spirit
has found complete usefulness.

Along with fasting, prayer, almsgiving, and dietary regulations, Thomas rejects circumcision, as most early

Christians did. A singular argument perhaps from radical Hellenistic-Jewish sources, is advanced against it; it is unnatural (elsewhere Thomas does not appeal to the law of nature). What counts is true, spiritual circumcision (cf., Philippians 3:3).

[55] (90.23–24)

Jesus said:
 Blessed are the poor,
 for yours is the kingdom of heaven.

Here Thomas combines Luke 6:20: "Blessed are the poor, for yours is the kingdom of God," with Matthew 5:3: "Blessed are the poor in spirit, for theirs is the kingdom of heaven." The "poor" are obviously Jesus's disciples.

[56] (90.25–29)

Jesus said:
 He who will not hate his father and his
  mother cannot be my disciple.
 And he who will not hate his brothers and his
  sisters, and carry his cross as I have,
 will not become worthy of me.

This saying is a combination of Luke 14:26–27 (hating father and mother, brothers and sisters, carrying cross, becoming disciple) with Matthew 10:37–38 (being worthy of me). From Luke, Thomas omits a mention of wife and children, perhaps because the Gnostic will have neither; he adds to carrying the cross "as I do" (or "like me," Doresse, page 177), perhaps because as in John 19:17, Jesus bears his own cross (Simon of Cyrene carries it in the synoptic gospels). A similar statement is found in Saying 98.

[57] (90.29–32)

Jesus said:
He who has known the world has found a
corpse,
and he who has found a corpse,
of him the world is not worthy.

Knowing the world is equivalent to finding a corpse (or, in the parallel Saying 80, a body); this knowledge and this discovery are evidently regarded as good, for the world is not worthy of the discoverer (cf., Hebrews 11:38, and page 77). Knowing the world, then, must be truly knowing it for what it is. But we must also consider one more saying (109). The world is not worthy of the one "who will find himself." We conclude that Saying 57, like these variants we have cited, is based on the verse which in Matthew (10:39; cf., Mark 8:34–35) follows the verses cited in Saying 56. "He who finds his soul [life] will lose it, and he who loses his soul for my sake will find it." Either Thomas simply mystifies his readers by speaking of a corpse or he uses "corpse" as the equivalent for "body" and hence for "self." The Naassenes used "corpse" of the spiritual man (Hippolytus, *Ref.*, 5, 8, 22).

[58] (90.32–91.7)

Jesus said:
The kingdom of the Father is like a man who
had [good] seed.

His enemy came in the night (and) sowed
tares upon the good seed.
The man did not allow the tares to be pulled
up.
He said to them, Lest you go that we may
pull up the tares,
and you pull up the wheat along with it.
For on the day of harvest the tares will
appear;
they will be pulled up and burned.

This saying is a summary of the parable found in Matthew 13:24–30, without any significant variants—except that Thomas substitutes "kingdom of the Father" for "kingdom of heaven." It is odd that the tares are allowed to grow up with the wheat, since the little fish are thrown away in Saying 7; but this problem is explained in the parable itself. Thomas omits the explanation of the parable which is given in Matthew 13:37–43, no doubt because he has his own.

[59] (91.7–9)

Jesus said:
Blessed is the man
who has labored (and) found life.

Here we find an equivalent, in the form of a blessing, to the invitation repeated in Saying 90 from Matthew 11:28–30; in that saying Matthew's reference to "labor" is omitted, perhaps in order to be placed here. "Finding rest" in Saying 90 is equivalent to "finding life" here. See also Saying 10, on "working together."

[60] (91.9–23)

Jesus said:
  Look upon the Living One as long as you live
    so that you will not die
    and seek to see him
    without being able to see (him).
  ⟨They saw⟩ a Samaritan bringing a lamb as he
    entered Judaea.
He said to his disciples:
  (Why is) he about the lamb?
They said to him:
  In order to kill it and eat it.
He said to them:
  As long as it lives, he will not eat it,
  but (only) if he kills it and it becomes a
    corpse.
They said:
  In no other way will it be able to become old.
He said to them:
  You too seek for yourselves a place within for
    rest,
  so that you will not become a corpse and be
    eaten.

The beginning of this saying somewhat resembles John
13:33: "Children, a little longer I am with you; you will
seek me . . . and where I go you cannot come." But the
story about the Samaritan and the lamb is apparently un-
paralleled. (The quotation from a Manichaean psalm
which Doresse gives [page 180] is related not to anything
like this story but to Christian exegesis of the story of
Abraham and Isaac as a prefiguration of Jesus's sacrifice.)
It may be that Jesus is the lamb, but the details of the
saying remain incomprehensible. More probably, the lamb

is the world (see Saying 6 and Commentary). Note that the "place" of rest is "within," as in Saying 25.

[61] (91.23–25)

Jesus said:
  Two will be resting on one bed;
  the one will die, the other will live.

This saying was probably attracted to the preceding one by the mention of "rest," and it gives a similar warning. It is based on Luke 17:34: "In that night two will be on one bed; the one will be taken and the other will be left." Apparently it leads toward the question of Salome in the next saying.

[62] (91.25–34)

Salome said:
  Who are you, O man? Have you as from the One
  mounted my bed and eaten from my table?
Jesus said to her:
  I am he who came into existence from that which is equal;
  I was given the things of my Father.
⟨*Salome said:*⟩
  I am your disciple.[9]
⟨*Jesus said:*⟩
  Therefore I say,
  when it is deserted, it will be full of light,
  but when it is shared, it will be full of darkness.

Unfortunately we do not know what Salome, prominent in the Gospel of the Egyptians, meant by her question,

[9] The form in Coptic is feminine.

or what Jesus meant by his answer, though it may contain reminiscences of John 5:18 ("He called God his own Father, making himself equal to God"; cf., Philippians 2:6) and Matthew 11:27 ("All things have been delivered to me by my Father"; cf., Luke 10:22). If it is the deserted bed which is full of light, we may have a reflection of the Naassene rejection of sexual intercourse (Hippolytus, *Ref.*, 5, 7, 13); see Saying 23 and Commentary.

[63] (91.34–92.2)

Jesus said:
I speak my mysteries . . .
. . . mystery.
Lo, what your right hand will do,
let your left hand not know that it does them.

The words, "I speak my mysteries," remind us of Matthew 13:11 and Luke 8:10: "To you it is given to know the mysteries of the kingdom" (cf., Mark 4:11); but the rest of the saying is too fragmentary to discuss. The final words of the saying come from Matthew 6:3.

[64] (92.2–10)

Jesus said:
There was a rich man who had many possessions.
He said, I will use my possessions
so that I may sow and reap and plant
and fill my storehouses with fruit,
so that I will have no need in anything.
Such were his thoughts in his heart.
And in that very night he died.
He who has ears, let him hear!

168

This is simply a revised version of the parable of the rich fool in Luke 12:16–20. The words, "This night they will require your soul of you," are omitted, perhaps because something like them will recur in Saying 88.

[65] (92.10–35)

Jesus said:
  A man had guests,
  and when he had prepared the banquet,
  he sent his slave to summon the guests.
  He came to the first; he said to him,
  My master summons you.
  He said,
  I have money for merchants;
  they will come to me at evening;
  I will go and give them orders;
  I excuse myself from the banquet.
  He came to another (and) said to him,
  My master has summoned you.
  He said to him,
  I have bought a house and am requested for
    a day;
  I will have no leisure.

  He came to another (and) said to him,
  My master summons you.
  He said to him,
  My friend will celebrate his wedding,
  and I will direct the banquet.
  I will not be able to come.
  I excuse myself from the banquet.

He came to another (and) said to him,
My master summons you.
He said to him,
I have bought a village; I go to get the rent;
I will not be able to come;
I excuse myself.

The slave came (and) said to his master,
Those whom you summoned to the banquet
have excused themselves.
The master said to his slave,
Go out to the streets;
bring those whom you will find,
so that they may celebrate the banquet.
The buyers and merchants [will] not [come]
into the places of the Father.

Here Thomas rewrites the parable of the banquet in Luke 14:16–24, adding some minor details from a similar story in Matthew 22:1–10. Much of the narrative differs from the gospel parables, however. According to Luke, the first man to be invited had bought a field which he had to see; another had bought five yoke of oxen and had to test them; the third had just been married. In Matthew only two are mentioned: one goes away to his own field, the other to his own business. As it is told in Thomas, the parable develops the notion of business dealings from Matthew, and the mention of a wedding (also in Matthew, but not as an excuse), as well as the recurrent sentence, "I excuse myself from the banquet," from Luke. The excuses offered in the Lucan parable reflect a rural atmosphere (field, oxen); those in Thomas seem to be more urban in character, and the idea of buying a village is alien to the environment of the synoptic gospels.

The parable ends with the master's saying to his slave,

"Go out to the streets"—as in both Matthew and Luke—
"bring those whom you will find" (Matthew 22:9; Thomas
does not like Luke's "Compel them to come in, so that my
house may be filled"). Thomas's conclusion resembles
Luke 14:24: "None of those men who were invited will
taste my supper." But he makes it more explicit by speaking of "sellers and merchants" (see Saying 92, where
taking interest is forbidden). This reminds us of the story
of the cleansing of the temple; Jesus drove out those who
were "selling and buying" there (Matthew 21:12; Mark
11:15—Luke 19:45 mentions only "sellers"—cf., John 2:14).

Thus, while the synoptic gospels are concerned only
with the fact that most men are occupied with worldly
affairs rather than with the kingdom, Thomas intends to
show that it is precisely buying and selling which lead
them astray.

[66] (93.1–16)

He said:
  A good man had a vineyard;
  he gave it to farmers
  that they might till it
  and he might receive its fruit from them.
  He sent his slave
  so that the farmers might give him
  the fruit of the vineyard.
  They overpowered his slave (and) beat him.
  They all but killed him.
  The slave came (and) told it to his master.
  His master said,
  Perhaps he did not know them.
  He sent another slave; the farmers beat the
    other.

Then the master sent his son.
He said, Perhaps they will reverence my son.
Since those farmers knew
that he was the heir of the vineyard,
they seized him (and) killed him.
He who has ears, let him hear!

This parable, like the preceding two, is derived from
the synoptic gospels (Matthew 21:33–41; Mark 12:1–9;
Luke 20:9–16), with a few additions, as well as the significant deletion of an allusion to Isaiah 5:1–2—"planted
a vineyard, set a wall about it, dug a ditch, built a tower."
This deletion seems to indicate the lateness of Thomas's
version, for Luke (who certainly was following Mark at
this point) has already left out some of the phrases derived from Isaiah. Thomas continues the process. As in
other sayings, he adds an admonition to "hear."

[67] (93.16–19)

Jesus said:
Instruct me concerning this stone
which the builders rejected;
it is turning into a cornerstone.

Just as in the synoptic gospels (Matthew 21:42; Mark
12:10; Luke 20:17), the saying about the stone which the
builders rejected is appended to the parable of the vineyard. (The Naassenes too were impressed by this mysterious saying; cf., Hippolytus, *Ref.*, 5, 7, 35.) But Thomas
deletes the synoptic reference to "reading" this saying
(Matthew, Mark) or to the fact that it is "written" (Luke)
—actually in Psalm 118 (117):22–23—because he is avoiding mention of the Old Testament. See Sayings 53 and 66
and Commentaries.

[68] (93.19–20)

Jesus said:
He who knows the All,
*   in that he alone has need,*
has a need everywhere.

This saying is incomprehensible. Presumably Jesus is
"the All," and "everywhere" is where Jesus is, as in Saying
77. If—as is most uncertain—the saying is related to Jesus's
words to Martha in Luke 10:41, "There is need of few
things or of one," it would mean that to know Jesus is all
that the believer needs. Perhaps the saying was garbled
during transmission.

[69] (93.21–24)

Jesus said:
Blessed are you when they hate you
*   and persecute you;*
and a place will not be found
*   where they have persecuted you.*

The first part of this saying is directly based on Luke
6:22 and Matthew 5:11; the second half looks like a reminiscence of Matthew 10:23: "When they persecute you
in this city [for Thomas, the world], flee to the other."

[70] (93.24–29)

Jesus said:
Blessed are they
*   who are persecuted in their hearts;*
*   they are the ones who have known the*
*   Father in truth.*
Blessed are those who are hungry
*   that the body of him who desires may be*
*   satisfied.*

173

Like Saying 69, this one is based on gospel Beatitudes. From the blessing on those who are persecuted (Matthew 5:10), Thomas turns to add materials taken from Matthew 5:8: "Blessed are the pure in heart, for they shall see God"; for him the vision of God is equivalent to knowing "the Father in truth" (knowing and worshiping the Father in truth, John 4:22–23). Then he goes back to Matthew 5:6 (hungering for righteousness, being filled), though with the parallel verse in Luke (6:21) he omits "for righteousness."

[71] (93.29–33)

Jesus said:

> *When you beget in yourselves him whom you have,*
> *he will save you.*
> *If you do not have him within yourselves,*
> *he whom you do not have within yourselves*
> *will kill you.*

This is a Gnostic version of the synoptic saying already reproduced in Saying 42. The Gnostic "begets" within himself the kingdom or Jesus or light and will be saved by what he begets; the non-Gnostic has nothing and will be killed by this nothing(ness).

[72] (93.34–94.6)

Jesus said:

> *I will destroy this house,*
> *and no one will be able to rebuild it.*

. . . . .[10]

---

[10] A new saying follows the lacuna. Some of the missing words probably were, "A man said to him."

Speak to my brothers
so that they will divide the vessels of my
father with me.
He said to him:
O man, who made me a divider?
He turned to his disciples (and) said to them:
Surely I am not a divider?

If the fragmentary remains of this saying have been
correctly restored by Leipoldt and Schoedel, it refers to
the accusation made against Jesus according to Mark
14:58: "I will destroy this temple made with hands." But
the restoration remains uncertain. A completely different
subject is discussed at the end of the saying, which is
based on Luke 12:13–14. "Tell my brother to divide the
inheritance with me." He said to him, "Man, who set me
as a judge or a divider over you?" The final question is
added by Thomas. Jesus is not really a divider (in spite of
Sayings 16, 56, and 98); he comes to restore man's lost
unity.

[73] (94.6–9)

Jesus said:
The harvest is great,
but the laborers are few.
Pray then the Lord
that he may cast laborers into the harvest.

Sayings 73–75 are all concerned with the contrast between the many and the few (see also Saying 24). Saying 73 is directly derived from Matthew 9:37; Luke
10:2.

[74] (94.9–11)[11]

He said:
O Lord, there are many about the well,
but there are none in the well.[12]

The "well" is the true well of spiritual water (see Sayings 12 and 105); many stand about it but few enter it to get the water. This saying was also found in the Ophite Gnostic *Heavenly Dialogue,* apparently known to the anti-Christian writer Celsus in the late second century; cf. Origen, *Contra Celsum,* 8, 15–16.

[75] (94.11–13)[13]

Jesus said:
Many stand before the door,
but the single ones are those who will enter
into the bridechamber.

The many who stood before the door are probably the foolish virgins of Matthew 25:1–13; they have no oil for their lamps, and hence no light. Only the wise virgins enter in with the Bridegroom. For "single ones," see Sayings 16 and 50.

[76] (94.13–22)

Jesus said:
The kingdom of the Father
is like a merchant who had a cargo,
(and) who found a pearl.

[11] A continuation of Saying 73.
[12] This translation depends on an emendation of the text. It was suggested by the close parallel in Origen, *Contra Celsum* 8.16: "How is it that many are round the well and no one goes into it?" (translated by H. Chadwick).
[13] A continuation of Saying 74.

He was a wise man.
(Therefore) he sold his cargo
and bought for himself the pearl alone.
You too seek for his treasure which does not
*   perish,*
which abides where no moth enters to eat
*   and worms do not destroy (anything).*

This saying is a revised version of the parable of the
pearl in Matthew 13:45–46. Since in Matthew the parable
is preceded by the parable of the hidden treasure, Thomas
adds a statement about treasure, derived from Matthew
6:20 (Luke 12:33). Matthew mentions moth and *brōsis*,
which means "rust"; Thomas takes *brōsis* very literally
to mean "eating," and therefore adds a word about worms.
The treasure is the inner man; what worms eat is the
body.

[77] (94.22–28)

Jesus said:
*   I am the light*
*   which is over everything.*
*   I am the All;*
*   (from me) the All has gone forth,*
*   and to me the All has returned.*
*   Split wood: I am there.*
*   Lift up the stone, and you will find me there.*

Jesus is the inner man; he is also the light of the world
(John 8:12). As in the Martyrdom of Peter (chapter 10)
and in Gnostic writings, he is "the All," the totality of
authentic being. The fullness of deity dwells in him (Colossians 2:9); in him everything was created (came into

existence), and he is the goal of everything (Colossians 1:16–17). For the Gnostic, this goal is not future but present. As the All, Jesus is everywhere present. He is in wood and under stones. We cannot agree with Doresse (pages 188–89) that Thomas is referring to the cross and the stone at his tomb. A much closer parallel is provided in the Gnostic Gospel of Eve (Epiphanius, *Pan.*, 26, 3, 1): "In all things I am scattered, and from wherever you wish you collect me." At this point Thomas's doctrine is pantheist, not Christian. The Greek version inserts the words about wood and stone at the end of Saying 31 to indicate that Jesus is present with his disciples, or with one disciple. The meaning is approximately the same: Jesus is everywhere.

[78] (94.28–95.3)

Jesus said:
  Why did you go out into the field?
  to see a reed which is shaken by the wind?
  and to see a man wearing soft clothing?
  [Behold, your] kings and your great men
    are the ones who wear soft clothing.
  And they will not be able to know the truth.

When the Gnostic is in the field, perhaps splitting the wood and lifting the stone of Saying 77, he is not looking for a wind-shaken reed or a king or a great man (in Matthew 11:7–8 and Luke 7:24–25 these words are related to John the Baptist—not so, here). Kings and great men "will not be able to know the truth"—contrast John 8:32: "You will know the truth, and the truth will make you free"—great men are enemies. See Saying 95.

[79] (95.3–12)

A woman in the crowd said to him:
    Blessed is the womb which bore you,
    and the breasts which nourished you!
He said to her:
    Blessed are those who have heard the Word
        of the Father
    and have kept it in truth!
    For the days will come (when) you will say,
    "Blessed is the womb which has not conceived,
    and the breasts which have not given milk!"

The first part of this saying comes from Luke 11:27–28, though the word "nourished" is derived from Luke 23:29, which Thomas uses as the second part of the saying. The word of the Father, then, is that sterility is better than pregnancy. Just so, in the Gospel of the Egyptians, Salome says to Jesus, "I did well, then, by not bearing [children]" (Clement of Alexandria, *Strom.*, 3, 66, 2). For Jesus really came "to destroy the works of the female" (*Strom.*, 3, 63, 2).

[80] (95.12–15)

Jesus said:
    He who has known the world has found the
        body,
    but he who has found the body,
    of him the world is not worthy.

See Commentary on Saying 57.

[81] (95.15–17)

Jesus said:
    May he who has become rich become a king,
    and may he who has power deny (the world).

Riches and power are characteristic of the One from whom Adam originated (Saying 85); they are given again to the Gnostic, who becomes a king (Saying 1) and, by knowing himself, escapes from "poverty" (Sayings 2 and 30).

[82] (95.17–19)

Jesus said:
 He who is near me is near the fire,
 and he who is far from me
  is far from the kingdom.

This saying is quoted by Origen (Migne, PG 13, 531D–32A) and, probably from him, by Didymus of Alexandria (PG 39, 1488D). For Origen's doubts about its authenticity see page 90. The fire is that which Jesus came to cast on the earth (Sayings 9 and 16); it is a symbol of the kingdom and therefore of the Father. We find something rather like this saying in the letter of Ignatius of Antioch to the Smyrnaeans (4, 2). "Why have I given myself up to death, to fire, to sword, to wild beasts? But near sword is near God, with wild beasts is with God." Perhaps Ignatius alludes to this saying; on the other hand, this saying may be based on the words of Ignatius.

[83] (95.19–24)

Jesus said:
 The images appear to man,
  and the light which is within them
  is hidden in the image of the light of the
   Father.
 He will be revealed,
 and his image is hidden through his light.

[84] (95.24–29) [14]

Jesus said:
> *The days (when) you see your likeness, you*
> *   rejoice;*
> *but when you see your images which have*
> *   been before you,*
> *they neither die nor appear.*
> *How much will you endure?*

[85] (95.29–34)

Jesus said:
> *Adam originated from a great power*
> *   and great wealth,*
> *and he was not worthy of you.*
> *For he was one worthy . . .*
> *. . . not of death.*

Doresse (pages 192–93) treats his equivalent of Sayings 83 and 84 together, but it would be better to treat 83, 84, and 85 as a unit. We begin with Saying 85. We know that Adam originated from a great power and great wealth because he was a copy of the "image" and "likeness" of God; he was both male and female (Genesis 1:26–27). He was not worthy of Gnostic believers, however, for he sinned—by increasing and multiplying, by being divided into male and female when Eve was taken from his rib. (Eve must return to Adam, as in Saying 112.) Apparently (Saying 84), men in general can see the "likeness," which they still retain. Not all can see the "images," for to see the image is to see Christ, which means to see the kingdom and, indeed, the inner man. This true image neither dies nor is openly manifest. At this time the image cannot be

[14] Perhaps a continuation of Saying 83.

seen openly or perfectly; it is fully seen only after death
(1 Corinthians 13:12, quoted by Doresse). Saying 83 explains why the image cannot be fully seen now. The
image contains light (see Saying 51), but this light is
overshadowed by the image of the light of the Father (cf.,
2 Corinthians 4:4, 6). Later, however, "If he is manifest
we shall be like him, for we shall see him as he is" (1 John
3:2). If this is what these sayings mean, Thomas has
expressed it rather obscurely, using image terminology
perhaps like that of the Naassenes (Hippolytus, *Ref.*, 5,
8, 10).

[86] (95.34–96.4)

Jesus said:
[The foxes have their holes] and the birds
have their nest;
but the Son of Man has no place to lay his
head and to rest.

Something has been lost at the beginning, but this saying is nothing but a repetition of the gospel statement
about the Son of Man and his life of detachment from the
world (Matthew 8:20; Luke 9:58). What is characteristic
of the Son of Man must also be characteristic of his disciples, who are "sons of men" (Saying 103). The place of
"rest" (Thomas adds "to rest" to the saying; cf., Sayings
51, 52, and 90) is not on earth but within.

[87] (96.4–7)

Jesus said:
Wretched is the body which hangs upon a
body,
and wretched is the soul which hangs upon
them both.

Since Saying 86 is a quotation from Matthew and Luke, we may expect that the present saying is related to something in the context those gospels provide (cf., Sayings 69–70). Indeed, it may well be a Gnosticizing interpretation of the mysterious words reported in Matthew 8:22 (Luke 9:60): "Leave the dead to bury their own dead." All earthly ties must be broken, as in Sayings 80 and 110. So Doresse, page 194. To know the world is to find a corpse (Saying 57).

[88] (96.7–12)

Jesus said:
> *The angels come to you, and the prophets,*
> *and they will give you what belongs to you,*
> *and you too give them what is in your hands,*
> *and say to yourselves, "On what day do they*
> *come and take their own?"*

Angels are the messengers of the Son of Man, e.g., in Matthew 13:41. They give man his true self, the kingdom. It is not clear what the prophets have to do with this. Perhaps the emphasis is on what men give the prophets, for "many prophets . . . desired to see what you see and did not see it" (Matthew 13:17; Luke 10:24). The day on which they come and take their own is presumably the day of death; compare Luke 12:20 (in the parable of the rich fool, Saying 64): "This night they will require your soul [life] from you."

[89] (96.13–16)

Jesus said:
> *Why do you wash the outside of the cup?*
> *Do you not know that he who made the inside*
> *is also he who made the outside?*

183

This saying, directed against ritual observances, is based on Luke 11:39–40. The reversal of inside and outside in the second half of the saying is also found in some early manuscripts of Luke, and in patristic quotations.

[90] (96.16–20)

Jesus said:
  Come to me!
  For my yoke is easy and my rule is mild,
  and you will find rest for yourselves.

Matthew 11:28–30, has a different order and some different implications. "Come to me, *all you who labor and are burdened* [Thomas omits the italicized words], and I will give you rest [Thomas changes this to "you will find rest for yourselves"]. *Take my yoke upon you and learn from me, for I am meek and humble of heart* [omitted], and you will find rest for your souls [selves]; for my yoke is easy and my burden [Thomas substitutes "rule"] is light." Thomas wants the invitation to be addressed to Gnostics, not to those burdened by the world (he twice omits "burden") and he wants the emphasis to be placed on the reward of rest, not on the yoke of Christ.

[91] (96.20–25)

They said to him:
  Tell us who you are,
    so that we may believe in you.
He said to them:
  You test the face of the heaven and the earth,
  and you do not know what is before you,
  and you do not know to test this time.

As in Saying 44, the disciples ask Jesus who he is (see also Saying 62). Similarly, in John 8:25–30, when Jesus is asked who he is and gives a reply, "many believed in him." The question they ask here is not unlike the request for a sign in Matthew 16:1 (Mark 8:11; Luke 11:16). The answer Jesus gives is a demand for self-knowledge; it is based on Luke 12:56–57 (parallel in part to Matthew 16:3). See Saying 4.

[92] (96.25–97.2)

Jesus said:
  Seek and you will find.
  But what you have asked me about during
      these days,
    I did not tell you on that day.
  Now I want to say them
      and you are not seeking after them.
  Do not give that which is holy to the dogs,
    lest they cast them on the dung.
  Do not cast the pearls to the swine,
    lest they make it . . .
Jesus [said]: [15]
  He who seeks will find,
    [and he who enters] in,
    to him it will be opened.
[Jesus said:] [15]
  If you have money,
    do not give on interest.
  But give . . . from whom you will not get
      them back.

"Seek and you will find" recalls Saying 1 but is directly based on Matthew 7:7 and Luke 11:9; it is repeated in a different form, from Matthew 7:8 (Luke 11:10), a little

---

[15] Probably a new saying.

later in this saying. The sentences which come immediately after the introduction seem to constitute a garbled version of John 16:4–5: "These things I have spoken to you so that when their hour comes you may remember them. . . . But now I go to the one who sent me, and none of you asks me, 'Where are you going?'" The disciples are to seek and to find; but they are not to make public what they have found. The holy is not to be given to dogs; pearls are not to be cast to swine (outsiders are dogs and swine, as the Basilidians taught: Epiphanius, *Pan.*, 24, 5, 2). Gnostics and Christians alike were fond of this mysterious saying (Matthew 7:6). Both Gnostics (Basilidians; Elchasaites in Hippolytus, *Ref.*, 9, 17, 1) and Christians (Clement of Alexandria, *Strom.*, 1, 55, 3; 2, 7, 4; Origen, *Homily on Joshua*, 21, 2; Tertullian, *De praescriptione*, 26 and 41) applied it to secret doctrines, while in the second-century *Didache* (9, 5) it is referred to the Eucharist, in Tertullian (*De baptismo*, 18, 1) to baptism. The Naassenes took it to refer to sexual intercourse (Hippolytus, *Ref.*, 5, 8, 33), but Thomas probably does not have this interpretation in mind, at least not here.

At the end of the saying (after a break in the text) we probably encounter something quite different. Those who have money must not trade with it or take interest (contrast Matthew 25:27; Luke 19:23); they should give it to someone else. See Saying 65.

[93] (97.2–7)

Jesus [said]:
  The kingdom of the Father is like a woman.
  She took a little leaven, [put it] in dough,
  (and) made it into large loaves.
  He who has ears, let him hear!

This parable about the kingdom of the Father, like the one which follows it (Saying 94), compares the kingdom with a woman. The original version, in Matthew 13:33 and Luke 13:20–21, compared the kingdom of heaven or of God with the leaven which she used. Thomas's emphasis, as usual, is on the action of the Gnostic, not on the work of God. He adds an injunction to "hear" (Matthew 13:43, etc.).

[94] (97.7–15)

Jesus said:
> *The kingdom of the [Father] is like a woman*
> *who carries a vessel full of meal*
> *and goes a long way.*
> *The handle of the vessel broke;*
> *the meal flowed out behind her on the way.*
> *She did not notice it,*
> *she did not know how to work.*
> *When she reached her house,*
> *she set the vessel down and found it empty.*

This parable also compares the kingdom with a woman; it is not found in the gospels. Perhaps its meaning is given in the parable of the secretly growing seed in Mark 4:26–29. Doresse (page 198) cannot decide whether it refers to the imperceptible loss of the kingdom or to the contrast between its coming and the woman's failure to notice her loss; neither can we.

[95] (97.15–20)

Jesus said:
> *The kingdom of the Father is like a man*
> *who wanted to kill a great man.*

He drew the sword in his house
and ran it through the wall,
in order to know whether his hand was
strong enough.
Then he killed the great man.

It is better to compare the kingdom of the Father with a man (as here) than with a woman (as in the two sayings preceding this one); see Saying 112. The parable vaguely reminds us of Saul's throwing his spear at David, in the Old Testament, but Thomas is not interested in Old Testament allusions. It is more like the parable of the king going into battle who first makes an estimate concerning his prospects (Luke 14:31). He who would find the kingdom must count the cost. If he is strong enough, he can slay the "great man" (probably the world; see Saying 78).

[96] (97.21–26)

The disciples said to him:
  Your brothers and your mother are standing
    outside.
He said to them:
  Those here who do the will of my Father
  are my brothers and my mother;
  they are the ones who will enter into the
    kingdom of my Father.

This saying identifies Jesus's true "brothers and mother" with those who do the will of his Father and will enter the Kingdom (Matthew 12:47–50; Mark 3:32–35; Luke 8:20–21). Ties with an earthly family are to be broken, as in Sayings 56 and 98.

[97] (97.27–31)

They showed Jesus gold and said to him:
  Those who belong to Caesar demand from us
      tribute.
He said to them:
  Give to Caesar what belongs to Caesar.
  Give to God what belongs to God.
  And what is mine, give to me.

The complexities of Jesus's discussion of the tribute money in the gospels (Matthew 22:15–22; Mark 12:13–17; Luke 20:20–26) are left behind as Thomas relegates what belongs to Caesar and to God to a place of inferiority, compared with the inner man, who belongs to Jesus. Note that God seems to be inferior to Jesus; see Saying 31 and Commentary.

[98] (97.32–98.2)

He who will not hate his father and his mother
      as I (do),
  cannot be my [disciple].
And he who will [not] love his [father and] his
      mother as I (do),
  cannot be my [disciple]
  For my mother . . .
  but in truth she gave me life.

The substance of this saying has already been provided in Saying 56. Here, however, Jesus explicitly states that he himself hates his (earthly) father and mother (see Saying 96). The repeated phrase, "cannot be my disciple," comes, like most of the saying, from Luke 14:26. What he said about his mother (who gave him life?) cannot be recovered from the broken text. Perhaps he said, as in the Gospel of the Hebrews, that his mother was the Holy

Spirit. The statement about loving father and mother may refer to loving the Father and the Holy Spirit. Verbally it is quite close to Matthew 10:37: "He who loves father or mother more than me cannot be my disciple." The sense is quite different, however. On "father and mother" see Saying 102.

[99] (98.2–5)

Jesus said:
   Woe to the Pharisees!
   For they are like a dog which sleeps
     in the crib of the oxen;
   for he neither eats nor [lets] the oxen eat.

"Woe to the Pharisees!" recalls many similar expressions, especially in Matthew and Luke. "Woe to you scribes!" occurs in Luke 11:52, a verse whose meaning is much like that of this saying (see Saying 40). The dog in the manger is, of course, proverbial, and it was proverbial in the second century, as we know from the Greek satirist Lucian (*Timon*, 14; *Adv. indoctum*, 30). The story is told as a fable of Aesop (*Fab. Aesop.*, 228, page 111 Halm). Its presence in these literary or semi-literary sources does not mean that it was unknown outside them. Thomas could have picked it up anywhere.

[100] (98.5–10)

Jesus said:
   Blessed is the man
   who knows that fierce robbers are entering,
   so that he arises
   and is prepared in his [strength]
   and girds his loins
   before they enter.

This saying is based on the parable related in Matthew 24:43–44 and Luke 12:38–39. The mention of girding loins comes from a preceding verse in Luke (12:35). See Saying 22, where the teaching is the same.

[101] (98.10–16)

They said to him:
Come, let us pray today and fast.
Jesus said:
What sin, then, have I committed,
or in what have I been overcome?
But when the bridegroom comes out of the
bridechamber,
then may they fast and pray.

Jesus is asked to pray and fast (see Sayings 5 and 14). Since he has committed no sin, he refuses, just as in the Gospel of the Hebrews (see page 33) he does not wish to be baptized, and in John 7:3–9 Jesus does not wish to go to the Feast of Tabernacles. However, fasting and prayer are permissible "when the bridegroom comes out of the bridechamber" (cf., Matthew 9:14; Mark 2:19–20; Luke 5:34–35). Since no Gnostic leaves the bridechamber (see Saying 75), this means that the Gnostic will never fast or pray.

[102] (98.16–18)

Jesus said:
He who will know the Father and the Mother
will be called "the son of a prostitute."

In John 8:42 "the Jews" seem to imply that Jesus was born "of fornication." They do not know the Father; Jesus does know him (John 8:55). Perhaps Thomas is referring to this passage and adding "the Mother" with a reference to the Holy Spirit (?).

[103] (98.18–22)

Jesus said:
   When you make the two one,
   you will become sons of man;
   and if you say, Mountain, be removed!
   it will move.

For "becoming one," see Sayings 3, 10, and 23; and for an explanation of this saying see Commentary on Saying 49.

[104] (98.22–27)

Jesus said:
   The kingdom is like a shepherd
      who had a hundred sheep.
   One of them, the largest, lost his way.
   He left the ninety-nine and sought the one
      until he found it.
   After he had toiled,
   he said to the sheep,
   I love you more than the ninety-nine.

This saying is based on the parable of the lost sheep in Luke 15:4–6 (Matthew 18:12–13), though in the gospels it is not a parable of the kingdom. Thomas rationalizes it by explaining that the lost sheep was the largest one; for this reason the shepherd toiled to find it and said that he loved it more than the ninety-nine others (cf., Matthew 18:13: "He rejoices over it more than over the ninety-nine"). Thomas thus misses the point completely. The lost sheep is apparently the Gnostic—or else it is the kingdom for which the Gnostic is to exert himself (see Sayings 10 and 59).

In the Gospel of Truth (cited by Doresse, page 201) the reason for seeking the lost sheep is different; $99 + 1 = 100$, a number more perfect than those from 1 to 99. There is no reason to suppose that Thomas has such calculations in mind.

[105] (98.28–30)

Jesus said:
  He who will drink from my mouth
    will become like me.
  I too will become he
    and the secrets will be revealed to him.

Jesus is the source of the water of life, as in Saying 12 (cf., John 4:14 and 7:37; Revelation 22:17); the person who drinks from his mouth becomes one with him, as in various Gnostic writings (Irenaeus, *Adv. haer.*, 1, 13, 3; *Pistis Sophia*, chapter 96; Gospel of Eve in Epiphanius, *Pan.*, 26, 3, 1: "I am you and you are I").

[106] (98.31–99.3)

Jesus said:
  The kingdom is like a man
    who has in his field a treasure which is
      hidden,
  of which he knows nothing;
  and [he did not find it before] he died.
  He left it to his [son], (and) his son knew
      nothing.
  He . . .d that field and sold it.
  [And] the buyer came, plowed, (and) [found]
      the treasure.

He began to lend money at interest to
[whomever] he wished.

This saying begins with words taken from the parable of the hidden treasure (Matthew 13:44; see Commentary on Saying 76), but it continues in a different way. Where the gospel parable says that the discoverer of the treasure concealed it again until he could sell everything he had and could buy the field where the treasure lay, Thomas tells us that neither the man who owned the field nor his son knew anything about it. The son sold the field to a buyer who found the treasure; the buyer was then in a position to make further gains by lending money at interest. Burying a talent in the ground is contrasted with lending it at interest in Matthew 25:24–27, and perhaps Thomas has these verses in mind. But as a whole his story is paralleled in a rabbinic parable of the second century (cited by Strack-Billerbeck, *Kommentar zum Neuen Testament aus Talmud und Midrasch,* I, 674) as well as in a fable ascribed to Aesop (cf., Garitte-Cerfaux, in Le Muséon, LXX, 1957, 315). The Aesopic fable is number 42 in the collection of Hausrath, number 98 a-b in the collection of Halm. Presumably Thomas has taken a current popular tale and assigned it to Jesus.

It is difficult to see just what it means to him. It might mean that the kingdom which the Jews, or people in general, could have known was given to others (cf., Matthew 8:11–12 [Luke 13:29]: "Many will come from East and West and will recline . . . but the sons of the kingdom will be cast out"). The "lending at interest" at the end of the story would then be spiritual, for taking interest is rejected in Saying 92. On the other hand, it might mean that unless you look for the treasure within your own field it will pass to others who will profit from it. The second interpretation seems more probable.

[107] (99.4–5)

Jesus said:
Let him who has found the world and become
    rich
deny the world.

This saying is probably a continuation of the preceding
one. The man who has found the world (to be what it is,
and thus has really found himself or the kingdom) and has
become rich deny the world. See Sayings 57 and 81, with
Commentaries.

[108] (99.6–8)

Jesus said:
The heavens will curl up and the earth
    before your eyes,
and he who lives from the [Living] One
    will not see death.

Like the beginning of Saying 10, this saying is based
on Matthew 24:35; Mark 13:31; and Luke 21:33: "Heaven
and earth will pass away, but my words [*logoi*] will not
pass away." The vivid detail about the "curling up" of the
heavens is ultimately derived from Isaiah 34:4, quoted in
Revelation 6:14. As in Saying 10 (see Commentary) the
logoi of Jesus are his true disciples, who have his words
within them. "If anyone keeps my word [*logos*], he will
never see death" (John 8:51; cf. also, Commentary on the
Preface).

[109] (99.8–10)

Did not Jesus say:
He who will find himself,
of him the world is not worthy?

This saying repeats the teaching of Sayings 57 and 80; see Commentary on Saying 57.

[110] (99.10–12)

Jesus said:
> *Woe to the flesh which hangs upon the soul!*
> *Woe to the soul which hangs upon the flesh!*

Flesh and soul are hostile toward each other; they must be separated, as in the similar Saying 87 (see also Saying 30).

[111] (99.12–27)

His disciples said to him:
> *On what day does the kingdom come?*
⟨Jesus said:⟩
> *It does not come when it is expected.*
> *They will not say, Lo, here! or Lo, there!*
> *But the kingdom of the Father*
> *is spread out upon the earth, and men do not*
>   *see it.*

Once more, as in Sayings 2 and 52, Thomas turns to the favorite text of the Naassenes, Luke 17:20–21 (cf. Hippolytus, *Ref.*, 5, 7, 20–21; 5, 8, 8). This time, however, his emphasis is not on the inwardness of the kingdom but on its presence among men. It is "spread out upon the earth," just as in Saying 2 it is both within men and outside them (Coptic; Greek has "within" only). It may be that Thomas has in mind the mysterious "sign of extension" mentioned in the second-century *Didache* (16, 6) as destined to come in the sky before the end of the world. Other second-century writers (e.g., Justin) find the "sign of extension" (the shape of the cross) present in nature. Perhaps this is what Thomas has in view.

[112] (99.18–26)

Simon Peter said to them:
    Let Mariham go away from us.
    For women are not worthy of life.
Jesus said:
    Lo, I will draw her
    so that I will make her a man
    so that she too may become a living spirit
    which is like you men;
    for every woman who makes herself a man
    will enter into the kingdom of heaven.

THE GOSPEL ACCORDING TO THOMAS

As in the Gospel of Mary (pages 17–18 of the papyrus) and in *Pistis Sophia* (chapter 146), Simon Peter is not enthusiastic about the presence of Mariham (mentioned in Saying 21), just as in John 4:27 the disciples of Jesus are amazed because he is speaking with a woman. Male and female must become one (Saying 23 and Commentary). Jesus will "draw" her (John 12:32) so that she will become "one spirit" with him (1 Corinthians 6:17). She will become a man; just so, Ignatius of Antioch says that when he receives the pure light he will "become a man" (*Romans*, 6, 2; for another parallel to Ignatius see Commentary on Saying 82). In order to enter into the kingdom of heaven, women must become men. We might be tempted to take this notion symbolically were it not for the existence of Gnostic parallels, for example in the Gospel of Mary (page 9), in Clement of Alexandria (*Excerpta ex Theodoto*, 21, 3), and among the Naassenes.

The "house of God" is reserved "for the spiritual ones alone; when they come there they cast off their garments [see Saying 38] and all become bridegrooms [Saying 75], having been made male by the virginal Spirit" (Hippolytus, *Ref.*, 5, 8, 44). The high point of Thomas's eschatology is thus reached, at the end of his gospel, with the obliteration of sex.

SELECT BIBLIOGRAPHY

Bell, H. I. *Recent Discoveries of Biblical Papyri*, Oxford, 1937

Bell, H. I.–Skeat, T. C. *Fragments of an Unknown Gospel and Other Early Christian Papyri*, London, 1935

Carcopino, J. *De Pythagore aux Apôtres*, Paris, 1956

Casey, R. P. "Naassenes and Ophites," Journal of Theological Studies, XXVII (1925–26), 374–87

Doresse, J. *Les livres secrets des Gnostiques d'Egypte*. I. Introduction, Paris, 1958. II. L'Évangile selon Thomas, Paris, 1959

Dunkerley, R. *Beyond the Gospels*, Penguin Books, 1957

Garitte, G. "Le premier volume de l'édition photographique des manuscrits gnostiques coptes et l'Évangile de Thomas," Le Muséon, LXX (1957), 59–73

Garitte, G.–Cerfaux, L. "Les paraboles du royaume dans l'Évangile de Thomas," Le Muséon, LXX (1957), 307–27

Grant, F. C. "The Authenticity of Jesus' Sayings," Zeitschrift für die neutestamentliche Wissenschaft, Beiheft, XXI (1954), 137–43

Grant, R. M., *Gnosticism and Early Christianity*, New York, 1959

Grenfell, B. P.–Wharton, L. D.–Hunt, A. S. *New Sayings of Jesus and Fragment of a Lost Gospel*, New York, 1904

James, M. R. *The Apocryphal New Testament*, Oxford, 1924

Jeremias, J. *Unknown Sayings of Jesus*, New York, 1957

Köster, H. "Die ausserkanonischen Herrenworte," Zeitschrift für die neutestamentliche Wissenschaft, XLVIII (1957), 220–37

Köster, H. Synoptische Überlieferung bei den Apostolischen Vätern, Texte und Untersuchungen, LXV, Berlin, 1957

Labib, P. Coptic Gnostic Papyri in the Coptic Museum of Old Cairo, I, Cairo, 1956

Lagrange, M.-J. "L'évangile selon les Hébreux," Revue Biblique, XXXI (1922), 161–81; 321–49

Leipoldt, J. "Eine neues Evangelium? Das koptische Thomasevangelium übersetzt und besprochen," Theologische Literaturzeitung, LXXXIII (1958), 481–96

Mayeda, G. Das Leben–Jesu–Fragment Papyrus Egerton 2 und seine Stellung in der urchristlichen Literaturgeschichte, Berlin, 1946

Osborn, G. "Note on P. Oxy. 655," Journal of Theological Studies XXXI (1930–31), 179

Puech, H.-C. "Un logion de Jésus sur bandelette funéraire," Revue de l'histoire des religions, CXLVII (1955), 126–29

———. "Une collection de paroles de Jésus récemment retrouvée: l'évangile selon Thomas," Comptes rendus de l'Académie des Inscriptions et Belles-Lettres, 1957, 146–67

———. See Schneemelcher, W.

Quispel, G. "The Gospel of Thomas and the New Testament," Vigiliae Christianae, XI (1957), 189–207

———. "L'évangile selon Thomas et les Clémentines," Vigiliae Christianae, XII (1958), 181–96

Schneemelcher, W.–Hennecke, E. Neutestamentliche Apokryphen in deutscher Übersetzung, I (Evangelien), Tübingen, 1959

Swete, H. B. The Akhmim Fragment of the Apocryphal Gospel of St. Peter, London, 1893

Taylor, C. The Oxyrhynchus Sayings of Jesus Found in 1903, Oxford, 1905

Till, W. Die gnostischen Schriften des koptischen Papyrus

Berolinensis 8502, Texte und Untersuchungen, LX, Berlin, 1955

Vaganay, L. *L'évangile de Pierre*, Paris, 1930

Van Unnik, W. C. *Openbaringen uit Egyptisch Zand (De vondsten bij Nag-Hammadi)*, Den Haag, 1958

Wright, L. E. *Alterations of the Words of Jesus*, Cambridge, Mass., 1952

INDEX

Aesop, 190, 194
Apocryphal Acts:
Peter (Martyrdom of), 79, 89,
137, 143, 177
of Philip, 76
of Thomas, 67
Apocryphal Gospel(s), 31–61
of the Ebionites, 54
according to the Egyptians,
36–38, 78–80, 143, 153, 179
of Eve, 72, 178, 193
of the Hebrews, 31–36, 53,
74–78, 120, 189, 191
of Mariham (Mary), 58–61,
197
of Peter, 40–47
of Philip, 19, 66
Sophia of Jesus Christ, 60
of Truth, 19, 38, 65–66, 96–
97, 193
"Unknown," 54–57
Apocryphon of John, 19, 60
Augustine (354–430, bishop of
Hippo in Africa), 90, 162

Basilides (c. 117–138, at Alex-
andria), Basilidians, 30–31,
83, 88, 145, 186
Bell, H. I., 54, 56–57
Biblical writings:
Genesis, 144, 181
Leviticus, 77
Ecclesiastes, 83
Isaiah, 88, 134
Tobit, 77–78, 124–25
Matthew, 21, 25–27; and
Thomas, 108
Mark, 21, 25

Biblical writings (*cont'd*)
Luke, 21–23, 26, 29, 46, 49;
and Thomas, 105–6, 109,
114
John, 21–23, 26–28, 57; and
Thomas, 109, 113–14
Pauline epistles, 23–25, 30–
31
Peter, II, 23
Revelation, 118
Bultmann, R., 114
Burch, V., 32

Carpocratians (mid-2nd cen-
tury), 94–96
Cathari (medieval Gnostics), 82,
149
Cerfaux, L., 8, 70, 194
Chadwick, H., 176
Church writers:
Augustine, 90, 162
Clement, II, 36–37, 143
Clement of Alexandria, 27, 37,
74–75, 89, 91, 120, 126,
147, 197
Cyril of Jerusalem, 32, 91
Diatessaron. See Tatian
Didache, 186, 196
Didascalia Apostolorum, 89
Epiphanius, 38, 63
Eusebius, 23–31, 91
Hippolytus, 38, 63; as source
for information about Naas-
senes. *See* Gnostics, Naas-
senes
Ignatius, 28, 36, 180, 197
Irenaeus, 31, 38, 64, 91–92,
139, 193